Praise For
The Three Melissas

This handbook is not only a must-have and necessary resource to assist families navigating homelessness but pushes each of us as individuals and a society to expand the narrative about homelessness by lifting the voices of three mothers and their lived experiences.

The Melissas bring focus to homelessness impact on them as women, their children, and their survival and growth through lessons learned. A huge thank you to the Three Melissas for providing a guide that speaks to the experience of family homelessness, the need for self-care, parenting through disempowering circumstances, and supporting your own empowerment through self-advocacy.

DeBorah Gilbert White, PhD
author, Beyond Charity: A Sojourner's Reflections on Homelessness, Advocacy, Empowerment and Hope,
Director of Education
National Coalition for the Homeless,
Washington, D.C.

Courtesy of GCS Homeless Services
and Community Support
Homeless_Services@gcsnc.com

Parents who are experiencing homelessness do not need our judgment or our advice. They need our help... This book should be available in all schools, shelters, churches, family agencies, and libraries.

**Jennifer M. Kassebaum,
Owner, Flint Hills Books, Council Grove, KS**

The Three Melissas: The Practical Guide to Surviving Family Homelessness is an ideal complement to traditional textbooks and research literature, for both undergraduate and graduate courses in social work, public policy, parenting/family relations, education, and psychology. This book provides a unique perspective on family homelessness, based on the lived experiences of mothers who have found ways to nurture and protect their children amidst desperate circumstances and "broken" systems that are meant to support families.

Although their insight is primarily directed to other parents, this book—as an assigned reading in college courses—can educate and inspire future professionals and policymakers to dismantle systemic barriers to equitable housing, employment, and education. I highly recommend incorporating this book into your curriculum.

**Mary Haskett, Professor Emeritus,
North Carolina State University**

I cannot tell you how much this survival guide is needed! The three Melissas are our experts, and they provide professional tips that those of us in stable housing never take into consideration. Two chapters into it I had two extreme feelings. First, I felt heavy hearted thinking about what our unstably housed brothers and sisters must endure and think through every single day in order to survive. It is easy to judge those less fortunate than we are, but I think this guide really gives the "professionals" working with this population the ability to walk in all three Melissas' shoes. Then I felt an overwhelming urgency to get this information out to our MV [McKinney-Vento] families in New Mexico as soon as possible because this information is crucial for maneuvering though nearly impossible situations. The guide also provides solid, practical information that really any human can use in their daily lives.

In my opinion, I believe that it is essential that all schools have this guide available for their families, students, and professionals! It is a powerhouse of essential knowledge.

Dana Malone, MA | New Mexico State Coordinator | Education for Homeless Children and Youth Program

Copyright © 2024 HEAR US Inc.

www.CharlesBruceFoundation.org

P.O. Box 914
Carlisle, PA
17013

ISBN: 979-8-9881816-8-2

All rights reserved.

No part of this publication may be reproduced, distributed, or transmitted in any form or by any means, including photocopying, recording, or other electronic or mechanical methods, without the prior written permission of the publisher, except in the case of brief quotations embodied in critical reviews and certain other noncommercial uses permitted by copyright law. For permission requests, contact dianehearus@gmail.com.

Cover Designed by Chad Bruce
Interior Designed by Max Donnelly
Illustrations by Bonnie Tweedy Shaw
Edited by Cheryl Dunn Bychek

Printed in the United States

The Three Melissas

The Practical Guide to Surviving Family Homelessness

Diane Nilan and Diana Bowman
in collaboration with
The Three Melissas

The Charles Bruce Foundation
Carlisle, PA

The Three Melissas

Contents

- Wait! Read this First!
- Who Wrote this Book?
- Meet The Three Melissas!
- Speed Bumps and Brick Walls: The World of a Single Mother Experiencing Homelessness
- What You Need to Know: The Three Melissas' Tips for Getting By
- 'The Kids are Passengers Along for the Ride'
- It's Like an Elephant on your Shoulders
- 'A Judgment-Free Zone' – The Importance of School
- Surviving Homelessness Becomes a Super Power –Words of Encouragement
- Remove Unnecessary Barriers: Recommended Policy Changes
- Final, Not Final Thoughts

Extras That Make This Handbook Even More Worthwhile

- Tip Sheet for Hosts: Sharing Housing with a Family Experiencing Homelessness
- Tip Sheet for Families: Sharing Someone's House When Your Family Is Homeless
- Resources for Parents
- Legal Problems: No Easy Answers
- The Big Picture by Diana and Diane
- References and Suggested Reading

Dedications

Diane & Diana

To parents experiencing poverty and homelessness who keep their children safe through their determination, persistence, and ingenuity, even when keeping on seems just too hard.

Melissa A

I would like to express my gratitude to my family members, including Diane, Elijah, Natasha, Jaylin, Davion, Jakobe, and Alanna. They have been a source of strength and inspiration for me. Their love motivates me to strive for excellence and never give up, especially in the face of challenges such as homelessness, insecurity, uncertainty, and poverty. I encourage others facing similar struggles to think creatively, seek assistance when needed, offer support to others, and persevere. Remember, hope and positive outcomes await you.

Melissa N

In Memoriam of Beverly, my beautiful mother. You fought to get back to me until your very last breath. You taught me that love has no bounds, other people's opinions of you are just that, and you taught me to rise up no matter how many times I felt defeated. Your love was a tough love, but it was solid and fiercely loyal. I hope this book allows me to share my voice, lessons, strength, and courage that you instilled in me. May it be a guiding light in the darkest of times. Just as you always will be to me.

Melissa T

To all the children of the world that don't realize the purpose and power they give their mothers, everyday. But for my Madison and Hanna, I would've stopped getting out of bed a decade ago. Thank you for being the air in my lungs.

Wait! Read This First!

When writing a book about homelessness, people with lived experience are the experts. Sadly, they face challenges getting a book published, much less marketed. When developing a survival guide for parents experiencing homelessness, co-authors Diane Nilan and Diana Bowman wanted not only to help parents in chaotic homeless situations protect and care for their children, but to provide a window into the world of homelessness through the eyes of parents who had been there.

Nilan and Bowman, two long-time advocates and homelessness professionals, have more than 75 years combined experience learning about family homelessness in the U.S.. For decades, they have provided invaluable information and assistance to communities, educators, service providers, and policymakers. Conveying the challenges of experiencing homelessness **while** raising children as well as providing tips to help families survive the resulting hardships has always been at the heart of their efforts.

The Three Melissas takes their mission to another level: engaging the experts, namely parents with lived experience of homelessness, *The Three Melissas* features three mothers, all named Melissa, offering poignant insights into the trials they've faced. These courageous moms also provide scores of practical tips and words of encouragement to support and inspire other parents who are facing similar challenges.

Who Wrote This Book?

Diane Nilan

Diane Nilan has worked in homelessness, since the mid-1980s. Nilan managed large shelters in the Chicago suburbs for fifteen years. In the process, she became involved in grassroots advocacy — focusing on raising awareness and implementing systemic change. She and other advocates met with enormous success, implementing the first state law passed to remove educational barriers and increase school access for students experiencing homelessness (Illinois Education for Homeless Children Act, 1994).

Less than a decade later, Nilan became integrally involved in incorporating the Illinois law into federal legislation, with the reauthorization of the McKinney-Vento Assistance Improvements Act in 2002. She left shelter work in 2003 to share her knowledge of homelessness and of homeless education laws. Nilan founded a new program, Project REACH, with the goal of training educators in 305 Chicago-area school districts on their academic obligations to students experiencing homelessness. She quickly gained a clear understanding of the knowledge gap keeping many educators from implementing the new legislative requirements or even recognizing students experiencing homelessness. Nilan knew students and their parents could improve students' academic performance but lacked the opportunity. With a desire to channel the wisdom of those with lived experience to educators and the public, Diane founded HEAR US Inc., in 2005. Consequently, she sold her home and possessions, bought a small motorhome, and began traveling to non-urban areas across the country gathering stories from students and their parents. This one-woman nonprofit began filming and producing videos featuring hundreds of otherwise invisible students and families. These films provided firsthand stories to countless audiences including elected officials and school personnel.

Diana Bowman

Diana Bowman, a longtime educator of students from impoverished backgrounds, began her work in the field of homelessness with the National Center for Homeless Education (NCHE) at its inception in 1997. Funded by the U.S. Department of Education, NCHE is the technical assistance center that provides information and assistance to state departments of education, school districts, and schools across the nation, ensuring that they identify children and youth experiencing homelessness and provide them with services and educational opportunities.

For 20 years, Bowman served as director of NCHE, championing the importance of education in providing stability, security, and hope for children and youth experiencing homelessness. After retiring from NCHE, Diana continued to work on behalf of children in unstable and homeless situations.

In 2016, Bowman wrote *The Charlie Book: 60 Ways to Help Homeless Kids* as a guide for people and communities wishing to support children and youth experiencing homelessness. She also served as a guardian ad litem to advocate in the courts for children in the foster care system. Additionally, Bowman teaches for the University of the People, a free online university that serves students from all over the world, enabling them to attain a college education regardless of income. Many University of the People students are immigrants and refugees living in impoverished areas of the world.

Why These Authors?

Both Nilan and Bowman hold the fundamental belief that schools play a central role in supporting children and youth experiencing homelessness and that education is the best pathway to a stable and self-sufficient adulthood. These women have devoted incalculable effort to the implementation of the McKinney-Vento Act, the federal law that ensures that schools and school districts provide the support that children and youth in homeless situations need to be successful in school. These advocates know that as the McKinney-Vento Act evolved over the years, it became much more than a set of laws and policies. It became the galvanizing force for compassionate educators, student support personnel, and educational administrators working to ensure that children and youth experiencing homelessness receive support at their schools and are linked to services in the community.

The Three Melissas highlights the role of schools and the school district homeless liaisons (individuals mandated by the McKinney-Vento Act who are charged with helping children and youth who are homeless to enroll and be successful in school). The work of these liaisons is a key feature in the way that schools support families during their homelessness. Unfortunately, missing in the professional development training and the reams of McKinney-Vento materials distributed to public schools nationwide, is the practical know-how of individuals who have survived homelessness. Nilan and Bowman know that the heart of that message can only be delivered by those with firsthand experience.

Authors' notes: Through this book, you will see references to students, parents, and families "experiencing homelessness." This phrasing acknowledges that homelessness is not a character description; it is a living circumstance. People are people first; their living conditions are secondary. The language is wordy, but the distinction is important, especially in a society quick to judge others on circumstances that are, in large part, beyond their control.

We also refer to "moms" or "mothers" when a more gender-neutral term might be preferred by readers. Because this book centers around three mothers, aka The Three Melissas, we are taking authors' liberty.

Meet The Three Melissas!

The Three Melissas (Melissa A from Illinois, Melissa N from Florida, and Melissa T from Kansas), are the featured experts in the book. How did we settle on these three women?

This is Diane Nilan. I encountered these three moms during my cross-country travels interviewing families for my HEAR US filmmaking projects. Since hitting the road in 2005 in my little camper, I met many amazing parents, children, and youth. I gathered inspiring and informative stories to share on film. Among the hundreds of people who shared their stories, three creative and resilient single mothers, laser-focused on the well-being of their children during and after their time of homelessness, stood out. Coincidentally, they were all named Melissa.

As I got to know these women, having kept in touch with them over the past several years, I marveled at their wisdom and strength. The idiosyncrasy of meeting three Melissas gnawed at my mind. One thing led to another and the concept of *The Three Melissas: The Practical Guide to Surviving Family Homelessness* evolved. I suspected, knowing that each of them possessed extraordinary courage and determination to pursue justice, that they would be willing to participate in this unique project. The result — this book containing survival tips for families experiencing homelessness, delivered by mothers with lived experience.

My co-author, Diana Bowman, shared my interest. We determined that we should work together on a book about families experiencing homelessness and together we made my idea a reality. My publisher, the Charles Bruce Foundation, agreed to work with us on this exciting, innovative venture. And, because each Melissa enthusiastically agreed to collaborate on this survival guide, Diana and I got busy conducting in-depth interviews with them. We followed those one-on-one conversations with a number of group meetings, bringing the women together via Zoom to discuss issues further. The feedback provided by them throughout the process was, as we expected, invaluable.

The Melissas' stories are unique, but their parenting drive is universal. Their survival tips are critical. In case you're wondering, The Three Melissas received modest stipends for their time and will reap additional benefits from the sale of this book. The most important outcome for all of us, beyond any modest renumeration, is the good Diana and I know the Melissas will do for people new to homelessness who may benefit from their experience and ingenuity.

Here are my brief, albeit inadequate, introductions of the three Melissas.

Melissa A

I met Melissa A in Illinois in 2010. Having lost her housing, she was staying in a suburban Chicago motel with her five young children. Twenty-two years old, she and her kids had been homeless for four years in the Chicagoland area. After spending some time getting to know her and her family, it was obvious to me that this mother had an uncanny sense of parenting and a tremendous love for her children.

She, like countless invisible mothers across the land, had been dealt a tough hand from early on. Her dysfunctional home life as a child likely had a major impact as she grappled with growing up in poverty and her own childhood experiences with housing instability.

A mother at age 14, Melissa A has given birth to seven children. Her youngest passed away when the baby was only three months old.

Despite hardships, Melissa A managed to find bright spots—good people in her life who believed in her and imparted valuable lessons when this young mother needed support and guidance.

Unfortunately, and not uncommonly, Melissa A had a string of toxic relationships that undermined her family's stability, leading to years of intermittent homelessness. She and her children frequently stayed in hotels or bounced around – lodging with friends, strangers, in her car, and occasionally at homeless shelters.

Determined to keep her family together, Melissa often juggled three or four jobs at a time. Transportation was a challenge with an undependable car. When working several jobs, the family would lose their eligibility for Supplemental Nutrition Aid Program (SNAP) benefits – commonly referred to as food stamps. Childcare presented a major challenge. Family members weren't the most reliable source of support, even when watching her kids, because of their own toxic relationships. A small group of friends ended up helping her in various ways, giving this young mom at least a little support and sharing invaluable know-how.

With an unstable childhood and no source of support, Melissa A needed to learn lots of lessons fast. Holding down a nine-to-five job proved impossible, so she had to get creative. She learned where to get help when she needed it and how to make her limited funds stretch. She also learned whom she could and could not trust.

She frequented food pantries and got help from local agencies when they had funds available. (Even with a limited budget, she's an accomplished cook). Unfortunately, some of those local agencies would not assist families staying in hotels. When necessary, this desperate mom resorted to stealing to feed and clothe her family.

Melissa A, with her bright smile and hearty laugh, gives each of her children the gift of love that makes them feel like they're her favorite.

Presently — as I type — Melissa A, now age 38, faces on-going serious problems. She's living in a house with five of her children, still struggling to make ends meet. Making matters worse, she's lost her ability to hold down multiple jobs because of deteriorating health and unreliable transportation.

Melissa N

Melissa N was the matriarch of the first family I met when filming "My Own Four Walls" back in 2006. She has two daughters and a son. The *Journal of Florida Studies* estimates that in 2004, Hurricane Ivan displaced 1.6 million people — nearly 30 percent of the residents in the path of the storm. Melissa and her family were among those relocated to a Federal Emergency Management Agency (FEMA) trailer. Melissa N eventually wrangled ownership of the mobile home from FEMA for a nominal cost. That trailer continues to be home for Melissa and her family.

Regrettably, the trailer park they lived in after the hurricane developed problems with the sewer system, and the county closed the park. Melissa couldn't afford to lose her trailer. She needed to relocate it. In a gutsy move, she stood before the county commissioners and successfully advocated for the county to pay for her to transfer her home to a small, privately-owned property outside of Milton, Florida. The arrangement at this remote location remains fraught with tension as her now-adult children have intermittently needed to come home.

Prior to the trailer, Melissa, now 53, and her children experienced homelessness for many years. They stayed in area shelters, her car, motels, and with friends. The two fathers of her three children have not accepted their responsibilities, leaving Melissa in a constant state of poverty and housing instability. At our first meeting, I realized that Melissa N would do anything for her children, encouraging them to be their best selves despite the variability in their lives. She has protected them like a mama bear even though their financial resources were irregular and inadequate.

While still at their first trailer park, Melissa's sixteen-year-old daughter, the youngest of the two, got pregnant. With a combination of tremendous determination and her mom's support, the teen kept the baby and managed to finish high school. Melissa's other daughter left to live on her own right after finishing high school.

Melissa's bad luck didn't start with Hurricane Ivan. When Melissa herself was only sixteen, her mother was murdered. The tragedy created problems between her and her father, causing a rift that left the young woman without his support. Decades later, things have improved between them.

Following her dream, Melissa attended an area university and graduated with honors. Hired by the county homeless coalition, she put her passion and experience to work. Not surprisingly though, her desire and ability to work were hampered by her need to care for her son who has autism. Melissa continues to advocate for her son's education. Now 20, his needs seem to be in constant conflict with a system that apparently wants to discontinue the services and support he needs and to which he is entitled. Melissa is determined that he will gain the skills he needs to survive as an adult.

Her son's ongoing needs, compounded by her need for a working vehicle, mean Melissa N must still take jobs that allow her flexibility, like performing cleaning services at construction sites or in rental homes.

Melissa now has four beloved grandchildren. Victims of systemic poverty, her daughters and their families stay with Melissa off and on when they, too, lose housing. Ever the mama bear, Melissa keeps a close watch on her grandchildren.

Melissa T

I met Melissa T in 2015, in Hope, Kansas — a tiny rural town in the center of the state. Melissa, now 50, points to her younger years, when she experienced severe trauma, as the beginning of her struggles. For Melissa, as with countless mothers grappling with housing instability and poverty, hard lessons followed.

A dental hygienist, Melissa enjoyed working and, for a time, life seemed normal. It wasn't long before Melissa's traumatic past led to fractured relationships. Alliances with the fathers of her two daughters disintegrated and, by the time the girls were six and two, Melissa and her girls plunged into homelessness. With no option, Melissa's older daughter went to live with her father in another town. Her younger daughter stayed with her.

Melissa and her youngest endured a series of desperate housing arrangements. They tumbled from friends to acquaintances, quickly wearing out their welcome as conflicts arose. Rural Kansas lacked family shelters or services, so Melissa courageously took it upon herself to stand in front of church congregations and plead for help. To no avail!

Melissa and her daughter bounced around, eventually staying with strangers. Known as doubling-up, desperately unhoused people often move in with anyone who will have them. A shortage of shelter and housing options led to several precarious and abusive doubled-up situations. Irregular and inadequate child support made it impossible to patch their lives back together. Bad credit haunted Melissa. The lack of childcare and want of a vehicle made employment haphazard despite her best efforts.

After a series of miscellaneous short-term cleaning jobs, Melissa accepted a live-in caretaking job for an elderly disabled man. In exchange for her help, he gave the two of them a place to stay. After settling in and despite her prior stipulation that sex would never be part of the agreement, he began insisting on intimate physical contact. The in-house predator pressured her constantly, creating a menacing environment that concerned Melissa so much so that she hid knives in strategic places around the home. With no viable alternative housing, she hunkered down and did all she could to protect her daughter. The desperate mom remained ever vigilant to escape his harassment while not losing their precarious living arrangement.

After months, and despite her "employer's" malicious attempts to sabotage her move, she finally qualified for subsidized housing in Manhattan, Kansas.

Still in her subsidized apartment, Melissa's deteriorating health and need to support her daughter in school have kept them on the edge of homelessness. Her best attempts at working – for an advocacy project that valued input from people with lived experience of homelessness – were thwarted when a collection agency pursuing Melissa for past utility debts snatched her paycheck before it hit the bank. Melissa, like so many unstably housed people, is haunted by past utility costs far beyond her ability to repay. Those debts have destroyed her credit and limit future housing options.

Today, Melissa focuses on providing support for her younger daughter, now in high school. The two still see her older daughter occasionally. This determined mother finds ways to maintain their housing, despite her extremely limited income.

In the following chapters you will walk several miles in the shoes of these three brave women. Have no fear — they'll be there to guide you.

Speed Bumps and Brick Walls

The World of a Single Mother Experiencing Homelessness

Diane and Diana have pulled together an overview of circumstances that will put you in the position of a person experiencing homelessness. If you're already there, you might find it marginally comforting to know you're not alone.

When you're a single mom, life's already difficult. Without a place to live, your challenges become unimaginable. Everywhere you turn, you hit speed bumps and brick walls. Your kids are your most important focus but, without a home, you and your kids don't know where to turn for help. Day-to-day survival takes up all your time. Few people understand what you're going through and no one seems to care.

That's why we've asked The Three Melissas to help. They know what it's like to not have a place to live. They learned the hard way how to survive homelessness.

Everyone's experience of homelessness is different, but a lot of it is the same. While your experiences will be different from others, you'll learn from authentic experts. Here are a few of The Three Melissas' general thoughts to guide you along your journey:

- Crisis management is a full-time job. Trying to find a safe place for your kids to sleep takes up most of your time –

especially because you won't always succeed. Feeding and clothing them is no easy task, especially because you can't even scrape up enough money for little things. Without a functioning kitchen you must rely on fast food. You cannot give up!

- When one thing goes wrong, often *all the dominoes fall at once.* Since you don't have money or other resources, you must patch together your family's existence any way you can. *With chewing gum and string,* if necessary. Your existence is fragile, so even when something minor happens, it tends to upend everything. Getting ahead seems impossible because it's difficult to save money for those WTF moments.

- Finding a permanent place to live is just about impossible. Your credit stinks. You don't have money for a down payment on a place. The rental offices charge for credit checks and you can't even afford to pay for that. You look for any affordable places but find nothing. You get desperate and swallow your pride, turning to family or friends. At first you think it might work out, but then you have to start *walking on eggshells* and tension builds. You try to follow the rules and keep your kids under control. Often the expectations are impossible or objectionable or both. A family friend propositions you and demands sex for a place to stay. You know you might be asked to leave at a moment's notice. As much as you try to avoid trouble, it happens.

Melissa T described a time when she and her daughter were living with a friend. Suddenly her friend's adult daughter told her to leave because "it's been long enough." Once outside, Melissa and her daughter were locked out of the house. Later, her friend would not answer her calls.

- Once you've lost one flimsy arrangement, you turn to other family, friends, or acquaintances. No luck. They can't let you stay because of their lease. Or because you've got too many kids. Or they've already taken others in and they have no room. Or because they've already taken others in and there are too many kids for the lease. You get *creative* and go camping. Or sleep in your car. Or find places outside that you know are not safe, but you stay there anyhow.

- Staying in shelters, the obvious solution, doesn't happen for lots of reasons. Many communities don't have family shelters. Or they're full. Or they don't accept older children, especially boys. Pets aren't allowed. The shelters may have unreasonable time limits or rules that are hard to follow. Most shelters make people leave during the day. This is a major hardship for you. You have babies, toddlers, or a child with special needs.

Melissa A told of a situation where her son needed emergency treatment in a hospital that required him to stay overnight. However, the shelter where they stayed evicted families who did not spend every night there. If Melissa waited at the hospital with her son, she and her children would lose their spot. Melissa chose to leave her son in the hospital *alone* to save her family's space at the shelter.

Fortunately, the hospital intervened with the shelter, and the shelter relaxed that rule. Melissa and her children were able to stay in the Ronald McDonald House while her son remained at the hospital without losing their space at the shelter.

- You realize that you'd have to be a genius to meet your family's basic needs like food, clothing, hygiene, and adequate sleep. Where will you keep your stuff? How will you manage to get, store, and prepare food? What happens when your kids get sick? Where will you go during the day, especially if you have young children? How will you travel to different agencies where you might get help (or not)?

- How will you get around? Public transportation takes money, and its rigid schedule creates challenges for you to coordinate rides. If you're lucky enough to have a car, it's expensive—gas, maintenance, insurance. Will you depend on others for rides? That's shaky at best. Melissa A recalled getting up before dawn to walk to a bus stop for work and returning by bus after dark. Although she was able to keep her job, she had to leave her children with other people for the whole day.

- Your society expects you to work but provides no help to find and afford childcare. Working becomes nearly impossible. You may have friends and relatives who can help, but these arrangements are often unreliable. If you miss too many days from work to care for your children, you'll lose your job. Melissa A missed work regularly because she was unsure of the safety of her babysitting arrangement.

- You're being judged. You are struggling to reach out for help because you know you'll be judged as an inadequate parent. People are eager to blame you because, *you're the adult*. Many people do not understand the challenges you are facing as a person experiencing homelessness.

> *Melissa T explained, "I've heard it all: I should have planned better, I should have made better choices." Melissa A shared that the relatives who watched her children would make negative comments to the kids. Melissa N recalled a situation at school where the principal told her child who had lost a book that she needed to be more responsible with her belongings.*

What You Need to Know
The Three Melissas' Tips for Getting By

The Three Melissas faced these challenges and survived! They want to help you by sharing some lessons they learned during their homelessness.

Sharing Your Living Space With Others (aka Doubling Up)

When you lose your housing, chances are you'll turn to family, friends, or others to stay for what you think will be a short time. You're lucky if it ends up being a short time. If you're reading this book because you've lost your home, then you probably already know. Odds are, you've experienced homelessness for lots longer than you planned or hoped.

Because you're dependent on others, you and your kids are feeling like a burden to your hosts. This makes your situation fragile. You're afraid you'll be told to leave at any time for any reason. Melissa A said that when they were living with another family, "We didn't have the luxury of relaxing, chilling, having opinions, or our kids having freedom in somebody else's domain."

Questions to Consider

- How long do you think your host is willing to let you stay there?
- What can you do to minimize the

disruption in your host's home? How will you deal with the overcrowding? With the inconvenience caused by sharing a bathroom and kitchen? With small children running around and making noise?

- What do you think your host expects from you?
- What can you contribute to the household financially or with other kinds of help?
- What will you need to do to get along with your host and host's family?
- What will you do if you and your family are asked to leave?

Melissas' Tips

- Be grateful. You are in a home due to the good will of the host. They should feel appreciated and valued for helping you and your family.
- Set boundaries. Living in someone's home can strain the best friendship or family relationships. Melissa N said, "A helping heart with no boundaries spells trouble." Remember to communicate with common decency and respect. It's important to understand from the

beginning what your host expects from you and agree on expectations and rules. Are there definite times when the host's family needs access to the bathroom? Will you eat together? When will your children need to be quiet? Will you need to help pay bills? If your host has children, you must acknowledge that two families with children living together is not an ideal situation. Ask what you can do to help it all work.

- You and your kids must be good "guests," causing the least disruption in your host's home. Melissa A shared, "When we could not use the bathroom to bathe in our host's home, I would keep my own personal rags in the car to use for washing up in public restrooms."
- Be alert! Watch for changes in your relationship with your host. Your host may say, "My house is your house." Can you trust that? Only until you eat the last cookie or leave a plate in the sink.

  You may be told, "You're lazy. You don't do your part." Or perhaps your host says nothing, but you'll know with the roll of the eyes and other body language that you are unwelcome. There is a time limit for people's tolerance. People will think you can read their minds, but you can't. What they don't see is that you're in survival mode. When you get ***the signal***, you'll know something has changed. If at all possible, you must communicate with your host and identify the problem.

- Clean up. Of course, you must clean the areas where you and your children are staying, but cleaning up after others as well shows your host that you are *doing your part*.
- Share your food and money with your host, even if you're not able to contribute much. Melissa A encouraged paying one of the family's bills if possible. "If you're making only $100 a week and getting food stamps but have no other income, you must still contribute what you can."
- Look for ways to help. You may offer to watch your host's children or fix dinner. Melissa N recommended, "Make things move smoothly; get along, accommodate, and respect."

  Melissa A would style her host's hair.
- Don't buy food in bulk. This might create storage problems, but this could also result in your food being eaten by others.

- Watch your kids. Make sure they are not in the way. Have activities on hand for them to do. If they are noisy or if you have a baby that cries a lot, take them outside for a walk. Melissa A said,

> *"Without a doubt, the biggest parenting challenge while homeless was keeping my child out of their way. [My daughter] didn't naturally understand why she didn't have the freedom to run around the house or just do what kids do. It was so taxing for me. I became very skilled occupying her hands and interests. I could make something out of nothing just to give my baby something to do."*

- Be agreeable and pleasant to your host and their family. All three Melissas strongly advised keeping your opinions to yourself. If your host thinks you are being difficult, they will ask you to leave. Melissa N explained, "It's a fine line between picking your battles or remaining silent to keep the peace." She cautioned, "Who's going down with the ship? Not the person living there." And remember not to think family relationships will save you, she added, "You can burn a bridge by being disrespectful."

Melissa A described a hard-earned lesson, "When I was 18 years old with two kids and homeless, I was able to stay with one of my mom's friends who had four kids. I bought cereal and her kids ate it." But then, "I said something and got kicked out. I learned to be humble. Both my host and I felt we were right, but it wasn't worth getting kicked out for."

- Always think about and discuss how you plan to move forward. In most cases, when you stay with another family it'll be temporary. It's important for you to have a plan and for your host to know that you are looking for ways to become more permanently housed.

- Expect the unexpected. Living in someone else's space can destroy friendships. People think they have taken you in because they're your good friend. Later they learn that the friendship isn't good enough to withstand that sort of pressure. It can seem like a set-up, but they obviously had good intentions, or they wouldn't have let you stay.

Still, that's small comfort when you are asked to leave. Melissa T explained, "I moved in with strangers three times; I didn't know what I was in for. They would pretend to be good friends. You have to figure things out along the way."

- Have a backup plan in case you must leave the home where you are staying. There are many reasons why you may choose to leave or why your host will ask you to leave. And there are situations where a shared living arrangement turns abusive or violent. You may need to arrange for a new place to go at a moment's notice.

Although you must work hard to make your shared living situation as easy as possible for your host, you should expect your host to treat you with decency and respect. Oftentimes, living with another family is an unfamiliar experience for both the guest and the host. While you must do your best to be a good guest, the host should be a good host if they welcome you to their home. You and your host should talk about how you can work together to create a suitable environment for you and your kids. At the end of this book are tip sheets for guests and hosts that can guide a good discussion to get everyone on the same page.

Staying in a Shelter

Many families experiencing homelessness spend some time in overnight or transitional living shelters. Shelters might be helpful as an emergency option, but they are not home-sweet-home. At best, shelters disrupt family routines and afford little privacy. Their rules and requirements help people live together in often-overcrowded settings, but the structure is far from hospitable. Melissa N cautioned, "Shelters are primarily focusing on the needs of the adults. Children's needs are not considered, especially their emotional well-being at this time." As an example, in the shelter where she stayed, children were not allowed to have friends over. "It was difficult to have a sense of normalcy."

Questions to Consider

- Where is the nearest shelter with available space?
- How do you apply to stay there?
- Do they have a waiting list? What do you need to do to keep your spot on the list?
- Will the shelter accept all the members of your family?

- Is there space for your children to play?
- What are the shelter rules?
  - » What is the maximum allowable length of stay?
  - » What times of day are families are allowed in the shelter?
  - » Are there work requirements for adults? What are they?
  - » Do adults contribute part of their income? What percentage?
- How many personal items can you bring and how will you store your belongings?

Melissas' Tips

- Know the shelter's rules and routines and follow them, even though they might be restrictive. When living in a transitional shelter, *pick and choose your battles.* You must conform to the rules even if they seem to interfere with your gaining independence.
- Clean up after your family. Don't leave snacks and drinks in the common area.
- Clean the common areas, including cleaning up after other people when needed.
- Watch your children and manage their

noise.
- See what services are available at the shelter. Are there counseling programs for children and adults?
- If you are not able to stay at the shelter with your young children during the day, find a place where you can take them, such as a public library.
- Make efforts to get along with others staying at the shelter. Know when to talk to others and when to avoid contact. Everyone there is highly anxious, and everyone has triggers. Be respectful, knowing that you are all going through a challenging time.

Staying in a hotel (or motel)

Staying in a hotel is expensive. Even though the hotel you can afford will be cheap by vacationing standards, it may be easier than other housing options because there are often no security deposits or background checks.

Hotels and motels have their own other advantages and disadvantages. On the one hand, you have a bed, bathroom, and usually a television. But it gets crowded fast. You'll have all your belongings crammed in your room. It's hard to prepare decent meals with a tiny refrigerator and an equally tiny microwave. Cooking smells can be offensive to other guests. Food storage is limited. People come and go in a hotel — at all hours — and no one gets to know one another. It is difficult for you to determine who is safe to have around your children. When dangerous situations occur with other residents or visitors, you and your kids might be at risk. Cabin fever hits hard and fast, causing everyone to get on each other's nerves. Privacy doesn't exist. Then there's the daily challenge: how can you afford one more night?

Questions to Consider

- How will you pay for your stay? How long can you afford to stay? Will you have to pay in advance? Will the establishment allow a grace period in which you can gather resources to pay your bill before forcing you to leave or will you have to find other options quickly?
- Will you and your children have an adequate place to sleep?
- Some low-budget lodgings do not supply clean towels and linen. Will you have a place to wash your bedding, etc.?
- Will you have access to a microwave and refrigerator?
- Are there common areas where children

can do homework?
- Is there space inside or outside for children to play?
- Will you feel safe?
- What happens when rates change, as they will during special events and holidays? You must be prepared for temporary evictions.
- If you have a pet, can you ask a friend to take care of it until you get your own place?

Melissas' Tips

- Use a web search engine to find good prices for hotels.
- Be sure to know the rules before you book. Some hotels require a deposit that may be hard to afford.
- Watch your children carefully since strangers are continuously coming and going.
- If you don't have a car, make sure your hotel is near public transportation or close enough for you to walk where you need to go.
- Get a hotel room with a kitchen, if possible, or at least with a refrigerator

and microwave.
- Bring your food utensils to the hotel because these are usually not provided. Also, most hotels do not have paper towels or dish soap, so bring these with you as well.
- Save the personal-sized shampoos and soaps to use when you are no longer in the hotel.
- Keep a cooler filled with ice to keep food fresh. If you are in a hotel without a refrigerator, fill the cooler with ice from the hotel every day.
- Don't use the phone in the hotel; the charge for calls may be expensive.

Stretching the Dollar

If you had enough money, you wouldn't be in your situation of not having a home. Your limited income means you're often *robbing Peter to pay Paul*. You will often go without so that your kids may have what they need.

Questions to Consider

- How much money do you need in a month to meet your family's basic needs?
- What are your sources of income?
- Where can you safely stash money for

emergencies?
- Where can you seek help?
- What can you do to increase your income? Are there creative ways you can earn cash?
- Are there ways that you can efficiently save?
- How can you juggle your finances, deciding which bills you delay paying and which bills must be paid right away?

Melissas' Tips

- Pay attention to how you spend your money. Fast food can be a money pit. While homelessness makes it difficult to prepare food, you will find eating out to be very costly. Melissa A said, "I had a friend that would be like, you spent $15 on McDonald's this week, what is wrong with you? And at that point I was just like, what? We're poor. No. She's like, no, you cannot spend $15. She was really stern with me, and I really appreciate her. To this day, I really do because that $15 a week was $60 a month, and that goes towards my bills."
- Pack lunches. "Every dollar counts, so before you think about going to

McDonald's to get a Happy Meal for your children, you need to think about stability and saving." Melissa A continued, "You literally need to pack your lunches for school or for your lunch break at work so that you won't waste any money."

- If you are unable to pay a bill, call the company and see if you can arrange to pay the bill later or in installments.
- Buy in bulk when you can. However, be sure you can store your purchases, especially your food, securely.
- If living in a house, watch the use of lights and power, and keep the thermostat low. Your host family will appreciate your thoughtfulness.
- Use coupons. Melissa A explained that she learned how to coupon from the Internet and couponing groups on Facebook. She has saved hundreds of dollars.
- If you have a car, plan to run errands in ways that will save gas.
- Look for ways to earn additional money. Check out informal jobs. Performing little services each day can help you get

by and get rent for the day. Clean houses and babysit for people in the community. Employ skills you may have like cutting hair or doing nails for others.

- Set up a checking or savings account, even if it is small, so that you will have some resources for emergencies and unexpected expenses. Avoid check cashing fees and other extra charges whenever possible. Credit unions are good resources.

Food on the Go

You know it's important to eat right, but without a regular place to store and fix food, that's a challenge. When you're living with others and buying food to have on hand, others may eat your food. When staying in a car, camping, or in a hotel without a kitchen, meal preparation is difficult. No matter what your living situation is, healthy food like fresh fruit, vegetables, meat, and milk are expensive or nearly impossible to find at food pantries.

Questions to Consider

- How much food do you need each week?
- Do you have, or can you apply for, SNAP (Supplemental Nutrition Assistance Program) benefits?

- Where are food pantries in your community? When are they open? What are their limits?
- Can you buy food in bulk and store it and keep it secure from being eaten by others?
- How will you store perishable food?
- Do you have a place where you can cook or prepare food?
- What meals and snacks do your children receive at school?

Melissas' Tips

- Avoid fast food restaurants.
- Use food pantries.
- If you have access to a kitchen, cook in bulk so that you have meals for several days.
- If you are sharing housing or living in a shelter, buy food in small quantities so that it can be eaten by your family quickly and will not get eaten by others.
- If you do not have a way to cook but have access to a refrigerator, get one or two days'-worth of lunch meat and salad ingredients.
- Keep foods with a longer shelf life — like

bread, mustard, peanut butter, and jelly on hand.

- If you have access to a freezer, cut up and freeze fruit so that it doesn't spoil.
- Use regular bread for hamburgers and hotdog buns; it's cheaper.

Clothing

It may seem like a little thing, but clothing is a big deal for families without a regular place to live. You and your kids have basic needs for clothing which change as the weather changes. That doesn't even factor in the need for you to look good for work, or for your kids to fit in with peers, or to avoid bullying. Kids grow, get dirty, and lose things. You may not have a place to store belongings and/or money to go to laundromats.

Questions to Consider

- Do you have only the most essential clothes to carry with you and store where you are staying? Are there clothing items, such as those your children have outgrown or that you no longer wear, that you can leave behind?
- Do you have family or friends who can pass along clothes their kids have outgrown?

- Do you know where clothing closets and thrift shops are in your community?
- Do your children's schools have clothing closets?
- Do you have a friend or family member who could store your clothes while you are without a place to live?

Melissas' Tips

- Find clothing closets and thrift stores in your community. Ask your children's teachers or school social workers about clothing the school may provide. Ask if they provide vouchers for clothing shops. Melissa A added, "Talk to the social worker at school; schools have these things on site; food pantries often give clothing vouchers; contact churches; ask for hand-me-downs from friends and family; don't be too proud to take used things."

- If you must store your clothes somewhere, pack seven days-worth of clothing to take with you. Your kids will then have enough clothes to wear through the week. Packing a week's worth of clothes is especially important if you are living in a small space or do not have a car for additional storage. You can pack a week's worth of clothes in a suitcase that you can take with you on a bus or other public transport.

- If you need to spend a lot of time outside, such as walking during the day or staying in a campground at night, be sure to have adequate clothing and shoes to protect you and your kids from cold and wet weather. You can never have too many socks!
- As soon as the kids get back from school, have them change from their school clothes. If they didn't soil their clothes at school, you can fold them and put them away. This way you don't have to wash them as often.
- Find a place where you can do laundry. Some hotels, shelters, and schools have washers and dryers. Ask a friend or family member if they would let you do laundry at their home. Handwash your family's clothes, if necessary.
- If it's winter, you don't need summer clothes, so try to store those at the home of a friend or family member. Switch out for summer.
- Be mindful that your school-aged children may be bullied if they lack

appropriate clothing.

Storing Belongings

In addition to clothing, managing your other belongings is a big challenge. When you lost your place to live, you probably had items that you couldn't leave behind—identification, important documents, family keepsakes. Items with sentimental value—photos, toys, etc.—are hard to part with, so you grabbed them on the way out. But what will you do with your stuff now that you don't have a place to live or a safe spot to store things?

You may have rented a storage space, thinking you'd only need it for a short time. *Big mistake!* Storage units are expensive, and if you can't pay, they will lock you out and toss away your things. Worse yet, they'll sell your stuff and keep the money to compensate themselves for their inconvenience. Often, you're storing things that you didn't have time to sort or toss when you lost your housing. Most people end up spending thousands of dollars just to keep "stuff" that's not important or valuable. Whittling down your possessions, early on, will save you big money. In this time of instability, you're under a lot of stress. Don't make it worse by keeping things you won't need and can't afford to store. Melissa N observed, "You never completely unpack. You keep stuff in boxes in case you have to leave."

Questions to Consider

- What are the most essential items that you must take to your temporary living spaces?

- What belongings are essential to store because they are meaningful – literally irreplaceable – or because you will need them later? What items can you discard?

- Where will you store your belongings? Will you need to have access to them while you are homeless?

- Do you have a safe way to keep important documents or family pictures as you move from place to place?

Melissas' Tips

- Ask a family member or friend to store your belongings. Melissa T recalled, "I had a friend who allowed me to keep my belongings in an outdoor shed. I'm grateful because I had a lot of pictures of my girls I had forgotten about."

- Keep only what you need. Melissa A advised, "You can't have too many things when you don't have a place. It's a hassle.

You will lose stuff, and you can't depend on people keeping your things in a time frame in which you are unsure."

- Make sure you can easily access important documents like birth certificates, Social Security cards, and medical records. Keep these with you as you move from place to place.
- Never store irreplaceable items in a storage facility. If you are unable to pay for the space, you will not get these items back. Melissa T lamented, "I lost all my family photos in a storage space."
- Keep a watch over your belongings. Belongings are often stolen. Melissa A said, "I slept with my money in my socks."

Reaching Out

On a good day, it's hard to ask others for help. These are probably not good days for you and your family. You are likely afraid to ask for help knowing you'll be judged (at best) or afraid your children will be taken away (at worst). You probably feel like a bad parent, with lots of shame and alienation eating at you. However, the Melissas all agreed that asking for help is critical for parents to access resources. You must overcome your fear and pride.

Questions to Consider

- What family members and friends might be willing to help you?
- What organizations, churches, or social service organizations in your community could assist you?
- How might your children's school help your kids and you?
- Do you have access to a phone or computer?

Melissas' Tips

- Having access to a phone is critical. Force yourself to make calls. If you are unaware of what organizations in your community help folks in times of need, call the Essential Community Services/United Way hotline (211) for information and referrals in your community. You may learn that no one can help you at the moment you call, but you can follow up later. Melissa T said, "Keep asking. You learn every time with each place you call; you learn what to ask for." She added, "If you don't reach out, your situation won't get any better. Ego went out the door with homelessness. I talked to anyone who would listen."

- Surround yourself with good people and form support systems. This is especially important if you do not receive help from family or have another personal safety net. Melissa A remembered, "I had people who would check on me. It's important to connect to other people – reaching out or being open to people reaching out to you."

- Don't let the local agency off the hook until they refer you elsewhere. If you get someone on the phone who says they can't help you, ask if they can refer you to someone who can or give you an organization or phone number. "You must be the squeaky wheel." Melissa N was adamant. "Don't take no. Push to find an answer. You need persistence. Dig deep, dig past your fears, trauma, and anxiety. Ask questions."

- Talk to ministers at churches. You might not get any help – but then you might! Melissa T said, "I stood before the congregation in three churches and asked for prayers and help – that's hard to do." She dedicated herself to this, in search of help. "You have to be completely open and honest, not only about the situation you're in, but about what you need."

- If you have school-aged children, talk to school social workers. Melissa T said, "I would speak to the school social worker and totally take advantage of any programs offered that we could use quickly." She detailed, "For example, free coats and shoes, snacks on the weekend, and counseling... They have more resources than you can imagine, but you must ASK, ASK, ASK! Most school staff never imagined that we were homeless because we didn't 'look' homeless and had clean clothes that weren't torn, so ask for help."

Being Grateful

This is probably the worst time of your life. It may seem like you're not getting any help. You're afraid you'll be stuck in homelessness forever. Despite these difficult circumstances, the Melissas emphasized the importance of recognizing the help and kind acts that supported them during their homelessness. Moreover, each noted the importance of expressing their gratitude and of returning favors in whatever way they could.

Questions to Consider

- Who has gone out of their way to help you?
- What are some acts of gratitude that you can do for them?
- Who do you know that needs some kindness? What can you do to help them?

Melissas' Tips

- Nobody is obligated to help you. Therefore, when someone goes out of their way, let them know that you appreciate them. Melissa A said, "I always try to do something for people who have helped because there have been many times that I wasn't helped. So be humble and don't forget where you were and try to stick together."

- Be especially appreciative of those who help protect your children. "If you know someone who will keep your child safe while you are away, cherish them. Don't take advantage," cautioned Melissa A.

- If someone does something nice for you, do something nice for them. Perhaps you could cook them dinner. Offer gas money to people who give you a ride even if they are going in the same direction as you are.

- Pass the kindness along. Little things matter. Melissa N offered a suggestion: "Say to someone, 'I'm sorry that you're going through this.' Listen to other people."

"The Kids are Passengers Along for the Ride"

Your kids aren't wired to endure the uncertainty, discomfort, and instability of homelessness. It'll be hard on them. It hurts you to see them suffering. You're going to face immense hardships and feelings of inadequacy and shame, which may create huge tensions within your family. You'll worry about your living situation and if you're meeting your children's basic needs. You'll worry which strangers you can trust among the many strangers you'll encounter at this time.

You'll move around a lot, often have one or two jobs, and you may battle for child support. Like the Melissas, your kids may change schools a lot and lose friends. This loss is felt more keenly through middle or high school. While you're dealing with the challenges of getting back on your feet, you might overlook the emotional and mental health needs of your children. Melissa N knows how that feels, "The kids are passengers along for the ride."

Questions to Consider

- How much time do spend talking to your children every day?
- How can you tell when your children are upset or stressed?
- What red flags do you look for to identify people who shouldn't be around your

children?
- Have you talked to your children about staying safe?
- Have you talked to your children about inappropriate touching?
- What counseling services are available at your child's school or preschool?
- What activities can you arrange for your kids to give them a sense of normalcy?

Melissas' Tips

- Give your kids an emotionally safe place with you. Let them confide and share how they truly feel at the shelter, at someone's home, or at school. "In hindsight, during our homelessness, my kids' transitions were hard and making friends was hard," Melissa N recalled. "My kids were physically healthy, fed, and protected. They attended school regularly and did their homework, but I should have pushed them to express their sadness. I didn't know they were being bullied at school. They held things in, and it's hard for them to express themselves now."
- Don't hide things from your kids, although it might not be wise to give

them the gory details. If you have good communication, they will tell you what they are feeling and let you know about situations that you should be concerned about. Have age-appropriate conversations with your children. *Age-appropriate* is a matter of judgment. As Melissa A knows, some kids can handle hard truths, some can't: "Open communication is critical even if your child is four-years-old."

- Be honest with your kids. Be frank about what you can and cannot afford – like extracurricular activities. Melissa A said, "If you're honest with your kids, they will learn about saving money. Also, being honest builds trust. My kids tell me everything. I have close relationships with my kids."

- Look for changes in your children's behavior and follow up on any changes you see.

- Protect your children from people who can harm them. Sometimes parents who are homeless must leave their kids with people whom they don't know well. Melissa A elaborated, "If a kid is crying or doesn't want to be left at a certain place, it is essential to figure out why. Someone may be hurting them, and you don't know. You always have to think about whether you should go to work or stay with your kid."

- Educate your children about appropriate and inappropriate touching. Keep the lines of communication open. If your kids are with a dangerous person — either someone who is watching them or living in a shared space with your family, get out! The stakes are too high.

  Melissa A knows that "a predator can be a person whom you deem as very kind or unproblematic, so you have to teach your children very young what is not OK, what places can't be touched, no secrets, and only safe games."

  Or as Melissa N emphatically put it, "If your kids are not comfortable [being left with someone], you must fucking believe them!"

- Be aware of negative comments that your children may hear from people who are judging you or them for being homeless. These comments can come from anyone who does not understand the family's circumstances, including family members and teachers. Critical and insensitive comments are not helpful. Educate your friends and family members about homelessness. Homelessness is a circumstance — not a character flaw. If they continue to malign your family, don't let your children stay with these people.

Melissa N reminded us, "This was emotional abuse. Some people think they are entitled to say things because they are giving you things."

- Be aware of situations where your children are being bullied and talk with them. If bullying takes place at school, talk to the teacher. Help your kids become compassionate toward others. "I would tell my children that when people are focused on you, they probably have problems themselves," said Melissa A.

- Try to have a sense of humor. Or as Melissa A put it, "Laugh to keep from crying; make jokes. Then your kids will not be scared. Help them keep their minds off the situation, even though you might be panicking."

- Don't hide your feelings from your kids. Melissa A said, "Tell them it's OK to be a human being. It's all part of life."

- Don't talk about adult issues around your children. Melissa T said, "I kept things separate from [my daughter] because I didn't want her to take on my problems."
- Never make your children feel like they are a burden.
- Look for counseling services for your children. Some schools or shelters offer counseling. Your children may need someone to talk to outside of the family. Your school social worker can help arrange these services.
- Look for ways to socialize your kids. Try extracurricular activities. Some of the best things that happen to kids are because of involvement. Try chorus and drama. Extracurricular activities are important even though they may cost money to participate (food, uniforms, etc.). Ask for help from the school for these expenses.
- Melissa T suggested trying to arrange familiar activities for your kids. "If my daughter could just have a play date, if she could go to somebody's house with people she knows, just familiar things would make her feel as safe as possible."

It's Like an Elephant on Your Shoulders

As a parent in a homeless situation, you carry a lot on your shoulders. You must manage getting back on your feet and attaining stable housing, but you also have to make sure your kids are provided for and protected. Experiencing homelessness is draining. No matter how cautious you are, you will be exploited on many levels. Odds are you'll become silent and numb. Melissa N shared that "you feel stuck — that nothing you can do makes a difference."

Even if this is the beginning of your journey, you're physically, emotionally, and mentally exhausted, but you need to spend time with your kids to reassure them that you can keep them safe and comfortable. You want to protect your kids from trauma, even though you're dealing with your own trauma. You are strong and resourceful, but barely getting by. Melissa T attested to this: "I've been strong all my life. I don't want to be strong; strong hasn't gotten me anywhere. I just want to be normal, whatever that is."

Parents, with or without a place to live, frequently sacrifice their needs to ensure their children's needs are met. Melissa T reflected, "My mental, physical, any needs were not on my priority list because I was in survival mode with tunnel vision until we got settled in our own house."

She continued, "[My daughter] was my focus while I'd tune everything else out. My greatest fear was her growing up to have memories of all these places and people in negative ways while I neglected her. I always fought hard to prevent that for her. I made the best out of the worst situations, but it's never enough."

One of the most devastating and damaging aspects of being homeless, particularly as a single parent, is accepting a roommate situation that quickly evolves into a sexual tug-of-war. A platonic relationship can become predatory when the host expects you to provide sex — whether or not the subject was broached before agreeing to share living space. You, as you've been told by The Three Melissas, must explicitly discuss the conditions of doubling up *before* you move in — but always know that these agreements can turn sour in an instant. "The sexual element is always there. I didn't know how to prepare for this," Melissa T cautioned. "They feel they are helping you, so you owe them."

Often it won't matter how much you say, "No." The person with the home has the upper hand, and that may lead to your exploitation and powerlessness. Melissa T expressed all too well, "You are super vulnerable. When you're under someone else's roof, you have no control."

Memorize this number: 800-799-7233, the National Domestic Violence Hotline. Sexual assault is assault. If someone you live with is forcing you to engage in sex for stay, that's domestic violence. Call for help. Then, when you call **211** for housing or other assistance, tell them you're not safe and that you've contacted the National Domestic Violence Hotline. It gives your situation context—sexual assault in your own home – aka domestic violence – is dangerous for you and your children. These numbers will give you a starting point for figuring out what you need to do, but the kind and amount of help will depend on the local resources where you live.

The Melissas understand that reporting sexual violence to the police will invariably result in you losing your living situation. They understand that you will often choose to tolerate an unsafe living situation because homelessness is unsafe, too. Still, many municipalities have additional housing earmarked for victims of domestic violence and this designation can help you qualify for that housing.

The Essential Community Services number, **211**, may provide basic information about possible local resources, but they are not prepared to discuss your situation with you or offer you advice. The National Domestic Violence Hotline has trained crisis counselors who will provide information about possible short-term resources. They can also provide thoughtful support and help you evaluate your situation.

Questions to Consider

- How are you doing?
- Are you able to address problems, take care of daily tasks, reach out for help?
- Do you have a friend or family member on whom you can "unload" and be vulnerable?
- Do you need professional help?
- What mental health resources are available in your community?
- Do you know how to apply for publicly funded healthcare?
- Do you need to get out of a bad relationship?
- What do you do to take care of yourself?
- Do you have attainable goals?
- Do you know where the local domestic violence shelter is?

Melissas' Tips

- Surrender to the process. You didn't get into this situation in one day, nor will you get out of it in one day. Melissa T urged, "Be patient with yourself. Just get to the next day."

- Take advantage of counseling services wherever they are available. You must deal with your own trauma. Melissa T noted, "There is a huge difference between conventional therapy, which is good..." Melissa T added, "But if you have endured trauma, trauma therapy makes a huge difference because it deals with the here and the now and how to move forward."

- Give yourself a break. Melissa N said you mustn't "let someone tell you that watching a movie or getting a cheeseburger is wrong. You can't fight a battle if you have nothing to fight with."

- Don't let another person have control over your life. Be wary of strangers who offer you a place to stay with no strings attached. Be prepared for sexual advances and plan a strategy to deal with them.

- When you are feeling exploited (sexually or otherwise), abused, and powerless, find someone to talk to. Always remember, you are not alone, even if you have to call for help. Again, the number for the Domestic Violence Hotline is 800-799-7233. Melissa N said, "Talking about it helps with healing; talk to people who have compassion and can relate to your situation."

- Don't let people take your voice. Advocate for yourself and others. You must believe that you can make a difference. Advocate for your needs and the needs of your children. Melissa T said, "Use those feelings of anger and being fed up as the determination to make calls or write letters or emails to get to a better place, wherever that might be for you."

- Remember that your children may not see the situation as being as dire as you do. Your kids will likely see you as an awesome mom.

- Be proud of what you are doing – it may not seem like much, but you are taking care of your children in drastic circumstances. Set goals. Setting goals, even very small ones, will help you see your progress.

- Leave toxic relationships. They will destroy you.

A Judgment-Free Zone
The Importance of School

It's not your imagination. And it's not just your kids. Children have a hard time when they're homeless. So do parents. It's a terrible experience for lots of reasons. When you move to a temporary place, your kids lose their friends, toys, and pets. They may be hungry at times when there's not access to food. They may not have the clothes they need. They can't play freely when they are in a new place, and they may feel like they are not getting the attention they need as you struggle to stabilize your family.

Most children experience trauma when they experience homelessness. Your children may start acting out, seem depressed, or be fearful. Their behavior may be a temporary situation, but it is worth paying attention to, even while you search for a place of your own.

Younger children will struggle during this time, even though they don't know how to express it. They've figured out something is wrong. They pick up on your stress and notice the change in routines. You'll notice their behavior has changed; even their physical health may change. They may be little, but their needs right now are important for their future development, so whatever attention you can give them is vital.

Especially when you're experiencing homelessness, keep your children in school. It is critical. This includes preschool programs. School is a place of comfort and routine for children. School provides a break for your kids from the chaos and uncertainty of being homeless. School provides a break to concentrate on your own needs and activities, so you can get back on your feet. While your children are in school, you know they are in a safe and nurturing place. Also, a good education is the best way to help children avoid homelessness when they are adults.

The McKinney-Vento Act

This is an important civics lesson that will help you and your children!

A federal law called the McKinney-Vento Act requires public schools and school districts to help children who are homeless. Remember, you may find yourself in a school district that isn't aware of its obligations. Remember what The Three Melissas told you: Do NOT be afraid to advocate for your kids.

Schools are required to:

- Enroll your children immediately, even if you do not have documents that are usually required for enrollment, such as birth certificates or proof of where you are living. If the school district offers a preschool program, it must enroll young children experiencing homelessness and extend to those children the same services as they do for young people who are not homeless.

- Help you get immunization records or help your children get the immunizations they need. In the meantime, your children must be allowed to attend school.

- Provide supports your children may need, such as free meals, tutoring, and special education services.

- Allow your children to stay in their same school, aka their "school of origin," which means the school they attended before you lost your place to live, if your homelessness forced you to move and if it's in the best interest of your kids. This is an important requirement because it allows children to keep their same friends and school routines at a time when so many things have changed in their lives. Also, they won't fall behind in their studies as often happens when they transfer to another school. These school-of-origin provisions also apply to public preschool programs like Head Start.

- Provide transportation for your children, including your young children in public preschool programs, to and from the school of origin while your family is homeless. If you find permanent housing, this must continue until the end of that school year.

- Change all policies that would make it difficult for children who are homeless to enroll in school and participate in all school activities. For example, schools must not charge fees and fines for things like lost books. They also are not allowed to punish a child for circumstances resulting directly from their homelessness, such as absences or tardiness.

Now you see why this law is so important! Sadly, too few people know about it. Stick with us. What you'll learn here will help you and can benefit other families you meet along your way.

Definition of Homeless

Homelessness, under the McKinney-Vento Act, has a much broader, more realistic, definition than many people, including school officials, might know. If your child fits any of the criteria listed below, they can get the services listed above. The descriptions and examples listed are not the exact wording in the law, but they will get you into a good place to better understand this important law.

The McKinney-Vento Act defines "homeless children and youth" as anyone who lacks a "fixed, regular, and adequate nighttime residence." ***Fixed, regular, and adequate*** are important terms.

- ***Fixed*** means a place of your own, where you rent or own, or where you know you can count on staying. Where your stuff is, too.

- ***Regular*** means that you can go to this place every day, not like a homeless shelter that has a time limit for how long you can stay there, or a motel where you're worried about coming up with the nightly rate, or the doubled-up situation where you're concerned about wearing out your welcome.
- ***Adequate*** means that the space should be safe. Somewhere you can stay that does not have features that are harmful like exposed wires, mold, or no winter heating.

The law also lists specific situations that are considered homeless:

- Sharing the housing of others because you lost your place to live. This includes the kids' grandma or other family members.
- Staying in motels, hotels, or trailer parks (in inadequate or poorly maintained trailers or campers, not decent house trailers, which wouldn't be considered homeless) because you have no other options.
- Staying in emergency or transitional shelters.

- Staying in a place that's not meant for people to live: like a garage, storage shed, etc.
- Staying in cars, parks, public spaces, abandoned buildings, substandard housing, bus or train stations, hospital waiting rooms, etc.

Getting Services with the McKinney-Vento Act

Now that you know the basics of this important law, how do you make it work so your children get the services they need?

Every school district must employ a person called the "homeless liaison." You can find out who this person is and contact them in several ways:

- The person should be listed on your school district's website.
- You can call the school district's main phone number and ask who the homeless liaison is.
- You also can search online for "homeless liaison for [your school district's name]".
- You can go to the website nche.ed.gov for the National Center for Homeless Education (NCHE) and click on "Find

State & Local Contacts."
- You can call the NCHE Helpline at 800-308-2145 or email homeless@serve.org.

Contact the homeless liaison as soon as you can — once you lose your home. Arrange for immediate services. Remember, the school district is required to comply. The homeless liaison may also refer you to organizations in the community that may help you. (Warning: sometimes the homeless liaison may not be adequately trained for their job, for a variety of reasons. If that is the case, contact the NCHE Helpline at 800-308-2145 or email homeless@serve.org.)

The homeless liaison can help you find a program for your preschooler, either in the school district or in the community. Many public preschools may be available to your toddler, such as Head Start, Early Head Start, Title I preschools, and state-funded preschools. If your little one has special needs or developmental issues, ask about testing, programs, or services through special education or the Individuals with Disabilities Education Act (IDEA).

When enrolling your child in a new school, or to start a new school year in their current school, you must fill out forms. Those forms may have a spot to indicate that you have changed your address—because you lost your place to live. Often, after this pre-screening, the school office staff will put you in contact with the homeless liaison.

Additionally, if you tell your child's teacher that you are going through rough times, their teacher may help you contact the homeless liaison. The homeless liaison will arrange for your child to have all the services they need and give you information on community resources.

Remember, teachers and other school staff are important resources to help your kids in school. You may feel uncomfortable sharing that your family is homeless, but you must overcome your fears. Most teachers and staff are understanding and compassionate. If you see that your child is struggling in school, is being punished for not having homework done, can't concentrate in class, or is being bullied by other children, you should talk to the teacher, school social worker, or school counselor and explain what is going on in your lives.

Often, teachers, administrators, and other school staff have been trained on helping children with various types of trauma, including homelessness. They will appreciate your interest in your child's education and your willingness to give them information they need to help your child function better.

Sadly, a growing number of families are finding themselves homeless. Don't feel shame! You are trying to help your child get the help they are entitled to by law. You can do this! Be strong!

The Melissas all agreed that school was essential for them and their children. Melissa N said, "The McKinney-Vento Act is empowering and provides protection for parents and children alike." The Melissas worked hard to make sure their children attended school regularly and did their homework. Melissa N put it succinctly: "McKinney-Vento was a saving grace. The kids stayed in school and made friends. School was the only constant in their lives."

The Melissas developed good relationships with the homeless liaisons and got great resources and support from them. You may want to stay in communication with the homeless liaison where your child attended school when you and your family were homeless. Melissa N's experience proves this: "[My kids' liaison] is my hub of information, peace, and understanding. She is a judgment-free zone. She will find help or tell me where to find help."

This is what schools can offer your children when you experience homelessness:

- Free meals at school.
- Resources, such as food, clothing, and school supplies. Some schools give food and/or gift cards to you and your children. Some schools send food home with your children over the weekend.
- If your children move to a different school or if they have a lot of absences due to homelessness, schools will help your children catch up and get tutoring, if needed.
- Schools offer counseling and mental health services for your children. Some schools offer services for the whole family.
- School social workers can provide information on community resources.
- When you move to a temporary place outside of your children's school district, schools will provide transportation to enable your children to stay in their same school, if that is in their best interest. In fact, they are required to do this. But you may have to remind them of the law. Believe it or not, some school districts don't comply because they are unaware. Advocate for your children and make the school aware!
- Some schools offer extracurricular activities that can help your children develop friendships, interests, and socialization skills. Ask to have your kids included. Schools must help your children participate in these activities.

Questions to Consider

- Do your kids fit the definition of homeless in the McKinney-Vento Act? (The homeless liaison will help you determine if you fit the definition.)
- Who is the homeless liaison in the school district where you are staying? Have you contacted this person?
- If you have moved out of your children's school district, has the school district helped your children stay in their school of origin, including providing transportation?
- Are your children attending school regularly and doing their homework?
- Have you asked your kids about any problems they are having in school?
- What problems are your children having? Have you discussed these problems with their teachers, homeless liaison, school social worker, or school counselor?
- Have you discussed setting up tutoring or extra-curricular activities for your children?
- Have you discussed preschool programs

that may be available for your young children?

Melissas' Tips

- Build rapport with your school district's homeless liaison. Homeless liaisons are an integral part of everything. Often the homeless liaison helps with tutoring, shoes, school supplies, snacks, after school programs — even Christmas. Melissa N found their help to be comforting. "They can help families reach out and feel safe."

- Talk to your child's teacher, school social worker, or school counselor about your circumstances. Be aware that not every person you encounter will be able to understand what your children are going through. Teachers can be important allies for helping your children. Nevertheless, The Three Melissas each noted that they had encountered teachers that were not very understanding. The Melissas recommended that you "trust your gut" about how much to share.

- If you encounter a teacher or other school staff that is not understanding, contact the homeless liaison to get them to talk to the teacher or staff member for help with a problem your child is having. Melissa N emphasized, "Homeless liaisons are absolutely critical. They provide a safe space; they can reach out to administrators as the 'middleman.'"

- Help your kids find places and time to do homework. If they are unable to do homework where you are staying, ask your children's teachers to arrange for them to do homework at school in after school programs or during lunch.

- Remind your kids that their main job is to do well in school. Don't burden them with your problems, even if that problem is with their school. "Children shouldn't be included or directly involved in adult problems," Melissa T said. "They will somehow think it's their fault and try to 'fix it.' So, reassure them that you have it taken care of (even when you don't) and their only worry is to focus on doing their best in school."

- Ask the school social worker or homeless liaison for clothing and shoes. Most schools or school districts have clothing closets or will provide vouchers or gift cards.

- Keep your child in their same school if

you find a place to stay that's out of the school district. This stability is important for your child.
- Talk to your kids about what they did in school. Be genuinely interested in what they are doing.

Remember: For more information on the McKinney-Vento Act and the services that parents who are homeless can request for their kids, visit the NCHE website (nche.ed.gov). You can call NCHE's toll-free Helpline at 800-308-2145 or email homeless@serve.org and get assistance when you are having trouble getting services for your child at school.

*Surviving Homelessness
Becomes a Super Power*

Words of Encouragement

No matter how you look at it, homelessness can crush you like a bug on a windshield.

Homelessness is so much more than not having a home. It's a hornet's nest of challenges that plunge you into despair and destitution, over and over, often for years. We could go on with the metaphors, but suffice to say: You will question your self-worth; you will wonder if anyone can be trusted; you will doubt that anyone cares. You will search for hope. Can anything positive be said about homelessness? Anything encouraging?

The Three Melissas, strong mothers now relatively securely housed, believe so. While their lives remain challenging, they have gained time-tested practical insights that will help you. The tools they acquired could help anyone in poverty, homeless or not.

That's not to say that you or anyone else would ever "get over being homeless." The Melissas describe a lingering condition that they call PTHD (Post-Traumatic Homeless Disorder). With PTHD, even though you pay your bills, you may fear eviction at any time for any reason, or worse – that you will lose everything. Melissa A said that after two years of being in her own home, she finally started hanging up photos and adjusting her behaviors to make her rental feel like a home. Homelessness will live in the back of your mind. Additionally, years of stress and sacrifice have taken their toll on the health of the Melissas, and may take their toll on you.

Nevertheless, the Melissas agree that they learned life lessons, tricks of the homeless trade that benefit them and their children. Tricks that might benefit you. Homelessness gives you a perspective on the world unlike any other. As Melissa A put it, "You learn lessons from struggle."

We asked the Melissas "What did you learn from experiencing homelessness?"

- "To see things from multiple perspectives. Things aren't always what they seem. I can see people's situations in compassionate ways." (Melissa N)
- "To speak out for myself. I am my own advocate. You have to put yourself out there and do what is best for you and your family." (Melissa N)
- "Different ways to communicate with others. There is a difference between hearing and listening. You can't change anything when you're not listening. I learned how to hear people talk without reacting. All voices are important. Homelessness is not that typical picture

that people see. I learned how to break the stigmas we all battle with. For people who haven't experienced homelessness, I can bridge the gap and talk to both sides." (Melissa N)

- "I think the best lesson for every human being is to start off poor. You learn to be humble and appreciative of little things. My kids know how hard it is to work for the American dollar; they don't feel entitled. Five years ago, my son was opening Christmas presents, and after two presents, he stopped and said, 'That's enough.' He's humble and appreciative." (Melissa A)

- "How to manage our belongings; how to determine what's important and what's not; what you need for the next seven days that you can transport on a bus if you don't have a car. You don't accept things from people that you don't need. But you also must protect the things that are the most valuable to you." (Melissa A)

- "How to coupon. When I had my first kid, it was hard to get a job. Couponing took knowledge and time, but I saved a lot of money." (Melissa A)

- "I learned that my kids and I would

survive. I no longer have any fear, just a sense that we'll get through this. Homelessness was devastating, but angels always came to help us." (Melissa A)

Don't be too hard on yourself. Homelessness robs you of your self-worth. Society judges you not on your strength and resolve but on appearances — whether your child has a dirty shirt. It's difficult to focus on the nearly impossible things homelessness has put you through and that you've overcome. Most people who haven't faced the enormous challenges you've faced have no idea how tough life is for families in your situation. Looking back, the Melissas have recognized some things that they didn't see in themselves at the time that they experienced homelessness.

So, we asked the Melissas, "What are you proud of?"

- "My strength, my ability not to give up. I kept on going. I never gave up on working for my kids' well-being." (Melissa A)
- "The resolve that I was able to channel in, being able to look beyond the current situation and see something better. I used that to empower myself. When you get someplace, you can encourage others

and be that advocate on the other side of the desk." (Melissa N)

- "I'm most proud (as a whole) that over the last decade, I never relied on a man, or used others. I took my kid to-and-from school daily over the last seven years and have been heavily involved with her schools and education. She's had most of the same friends for years, and I put off personal relationships until she's grown, in a proactive way, so she never felt second best to mom!" (Melissa T)

As much as the Melissas wanted to share their survival tips for homelessness, they wanted to encourage you to find your own strength and voice. Melissa N advised, "It's important not to forget that each of our experiences individually and collectively matters. We must find a way to let people know so that things can change."

You won't be able to stop others from condemning you for what they see as your failures and mistakes. But don't lose sight of your incredible accomplishments in the face of horrible circumstances. Find strength in your accomplishments. Give voice to these accomplishments and others will see you in a new light as well.

"A lot of people don't understand when you say never give up. People think that others just say that, but it's coming from me. I'm a person that thought that I wanted to give up many times. I thought that it would never get better, but it will get better. You just got to stay focused and you got to dream high and never let your dreams be deflated because people say you can't or you won't, or something is always stopping you.

"And so, when I'm down on my luck, I always try to think 'This is not where I'm supposed to be,' even though it feels like I tried everything. I'm doing the right thing. I'm doing everything I can. It might take a couple days and more struggling, but there's going to be a better opportunity for you. So just keep your head held high and never give up, and make sure that you are the best inspiration for your child."

Melissa A

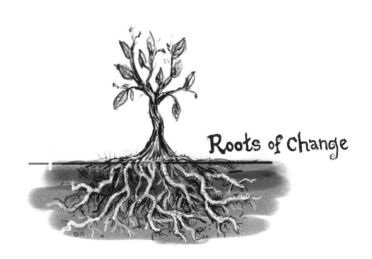

Remove Unnecessary Barriers
Recommended Policy Changes

The Melissas' willingness to share their observations, suggestions, and vulnerability for this project contributes invaluable information and inspiration that will benefit countless families for years to come. In addition to their survival suggestions for others who find themselves experiencing homelessness, our sheroes have compiled a list of things that could and should be changed.

Align Services With Needs

Many unnecessary barriers faced by parents who are homeless are the result of rules and policies in service organizations that do not meet the needs of these families. Rules and regulations typically prioritize only the efficient operation of organizations, not the people they serve. Additionally, the lack of alignment between policies and interpersonal needs stems from erroneous —often prejudiced — attitudes toward people who are homeless. A lack of understanding by shelter providers as well as housing case managers compounds the day-to-day challenges they face and increases their burdens.

Many challenges The Three Melissas faced during their homelessness resulted from rules and policies in service organizations that made their survival more difficult. The

Melissas highlighted a few situations they experienced where the services reflected a lack of understanding of the needs of people experiencing homelessness.

- A well-known charity solicited donations from the community at Christmas time and then provided $10.00 gift cards to the people who were homeless. "These gift cards were a joke!" Melissa A exclaimed. "These organizations get a lot of money, but they need a greater understanding of homelessness. They will give presents, but not help with basic needs, such as rent. They also make families jump through hoops to get help."

- Some agencies will not give food or money to people who are staying in a hotel because they think if they can afford a hotel, they must not have a great need. In reality, families who stay in hotels may be facing dire emergencies, fleeing a domestic violence situation, or not have enough money for a rental deposit. Staying in a hotel, even a low-rent hotel, which can be crowded and dangerous, quickly depletes any savings a family has.

- When distributing food, organizations

often do not consider where the family is living. For example, if the family is living in a hotel or in their car, they may not have an opportunity to prepare bulk foodstuffs.

Folks experiencing homelessness may often lack common necessities such as a can opener or a place to store perishable food. The organizations providing perishables should also provide the family with a cooler.

Change Attitudes and Offer Sensitivity Training

The Three Melissas have observed a great lack of compassion among service providers that stems from a lack of understanding of what families experiencing homelessness face.

Support systems are seldom realistic about the time it takes for families to become stabilized. Melissa N observed, "People think that, oh, well if this family didn't get it right in three weeks, six months, or if you're not meeting their timeframe and their mile markers, you're just not ever going to get it. They're not looking at what you've been through. They're not looking at the root. And that's what we need to understand is that there is a root." Homelessness is not a one-size-fits-all condition, and each family's complex circumstances defy simple and short-term solutions.

Support service staff frequently assume that families should be able to seek help from family and friends. Melissa N said, "Oh my gosh, how many times I was told, 'well, don't you have parents? Don't you have grandparents? Don't you have friends? Don't you have somebody who can help you?' And they think that it's okay to say that when we're sitting here knowing, yeah, I have them, but that's not a source that I can access for one reason or another. And everybody has a different story as to why they can or can't access that resource, but it's not because we don't want to. So, I think that's what they're not understanding is we are doing the best we can with what we have, and we are putting our kids first in the only ways that we know how."

The Melissas noted that judgment comes in many forms, from someone suggesting that you should be more organized to questioning why you don't get a job. Don't be surprised if people make offhanded comments to your children — even adults who you would think would know better. Teachers may punish your children for not having their homework completed.

The Melissas constantly experienced

judgment from family members, teachers, and service providers; it wore them down. They noted that people who work in educational and service organizations or in agencies for SNAP, Medicaid, or disability benefits can be rude and cynical. They may talk down to you in front of your kids. "People who ask for help don't want to be talked to in a condescending way." Melissa N said that when she encounters judgment or condescension, she feels like asking, "Why don't you come and do what I do for a day?"

"If you are traumatized and are struggling and have kids, children are your core – you provide and protect," Melissa N explained. "We need to create awareness on this aspect; people don't see this. They see us hustling. When you come home, you are not strong. What they see on the outside is not what's on the inside."

The Melissas believe that organizations should train employees and volunteers to help them understand what homelessness is like, to dispel the assumptions and preconceptions, and to reinforce that everyone should be treated with respect.

Learn from Those with Lived Experience to Improve Services

Even though services are well-intended, they may not be effective or useful when they don't match the reality. If an agency doesn't understand the needs of people experiencing homelessness, how can they provide assistance? The Three Melissas will tell you, "They can't."

The best way to ensure that services meet the needs is to involve people with lived experience of homelessness in developing these services. Melissa N, who worked for her county's homeless coalition, said that if you haven't been homeless, you can't truly understand what homelessness is like. In her position, she said she was able to have input in ways never before seen. She said, "We all have something to bring to the table, and there are some skills that can't be taught."

Melissa A recommended that employers weigh life experiences in the employment process: "I want to help people in my situation. I know how to help. Degrees can get in the way of people with experience and heart."

Support Victims of Domestic Abuse

Domestic violence victims need extensive support. Melissa T described a time when she called a domestic violence helpline but found no support after the initial call. She was referred to the only homeless shelter in the community, which was for men and women. She was on her own with a small child. She said, "There were people to reach out to but no 'after plan.' There isn't really any help; people think there is from the commercials. Women take the leap to leave and then there's no help. What are they supposed to do? When you have no friends and no vehicle, you're screwed."

Make Shelter Policies More Flexible

Shelters can be a lifeline when you are homeless. However, shelters often create additional challenges for residents, particularly single parents with small children. Following are the Melissas' recommendations for revising shelter rules and policies:

- Allow parents with small children or a sick child to stay in the shelter during the day. Shelters that cater to working adults usually allow people to stay at the shelter only from evening to early morning. A parent with a toddler must find a public space to stay in when residents are asked to leave each morning. This is exceptionally difficult when a child is sick and a parent must find a place to keep their child during the day.
- Have flexible curfews. Shelters with

strict curfews do not accommodate parents who have shift work that ends after regular operating hours. Melissa A observed "So even though people think you should work nine to five, sometimes working at night is more beneficial. If you're working in a warehouse or in a shift job, the overnight jobs usually pay more than the day shifts. You can save more money."

Shelters also give families' beds away when they do not show up for one or two evenings. Yet sometimes unexpected circumstances, such as a hospitalization for yourself or your child, can make this impossible. Shelters should review people's circumstances on a case-by-case basis.

- Keep families together. Some shelters will not allow fathers or children older than 12 years of age to stay with their families. In addition to the challenge parents face with making other arrangements, Melissa N suggested that this can make a teenager feel that they don't matter. Same-sex couples often face similar barriers.

- Provide childcare – or childcare support. Melissa N said that she was once called for a job interview but didn't have childcare and could not go. Parents also miss work when children are ill. These barriers to employment add more stress to the life of a parent who is homeless and is "just trying to make everything work."

- Provide secure lock boxes for families. Melissa A explained, "In a shelter, things get stolen. I've been robbed many times." If a family does not have a car or trustworthy people to leave belongings with, a place to store valuable items and documents is essential.

- Provide food and meals to families. Anyone going to a shelter has limited resources – or none. Providing meals or groceries saves money.

- Offer classes for residents, such as budgeting and couponing classes. Provide safety classes for kids. Help parents learn to set safe boundaries to keep them from being victimized. "We put ourselves in a position to protect our children but **we** need to learn that it's OK to say no." Melissa N added, "Mothers need a stronger foundation for when they get out of the shelter."

- Create a sense of normalcy. Transitional shelters have many rules. For example, you or your children may not be allowed to have friends over at certain times or watch certain movies. Some transitional shelters require you to provide a portion of your paycheck to the shelter.

Change How HUD Defines Homeless

The definition of homeless created by the U.S. Department of Housing and Urban Development (HUD) does not include families living in hotels/motels and in doubled-up situations due to loss of their housing. Many agencies and organizations use the HUD definition to determine who is eligible for services. As a result, families living in doubled-up situations don't qualify for help. Yet, living doubled up — or in fleabag motels — is often an unstable and precarious living situation. The Melissas suggest that the HUD definition should be broadened to match the definition in the McKinney-Vento Act so that services can be extended to those who are living in doubled-up situations or hotels/motels due to loss of housing.

Increase Services in Rural Communities

At some point during their homelessness, each of the Melissas lived in rural communities that lacked sufficient services for families experiencing homelessness. These regions lacked affordable housing, shelters, and transportation. Many families facing homelessness in rural areas must live in inadequate or dangerous situations. Additionally, parents who don't have cars cannot easily access jobs or services. People who lose their housing become the *hidden homeless.* Or as Melissa N puts it: "People don't see us; out of sight, out of mind."

While there are no easy answers to these challenges, rural communities should be aware that parents with children may need help but often remain unidentified. Town councils should address homelessness in their broad planning initiatives. Municipalities should create affordable housing, which may require them to look beyond approving only high-end housing developments or requiring those developments to build affordably priced housing as part of their approval.

In Summary

Although these recommendations address only a few of the challenges families experiencing homelessness face, let's recap the Melissas' recommendations that service providers should consider when setting policies and rules:

- Treat families with dignity and respect.
- Ensure all staff members are trained in understanding homelessness and in ways that help trauma-impacted people.
- Solicit input on policies from those with lived experience of homelessness.
- Ensure that financial support is of an amount that will make a difference.
- Make shelters hubs of support for parents with children. Families have very different needs from single adults.
- Provide a continuum of support to victims of domestic violence. A great deal is required beyond the first phone call.
- Provide support to single parents seeking and maintaining employment while caring for their children.
- Provide support for families living in hotels/motels and in doubled-up situations.
- While working with parents, acknowledge their strengths and address their trauma.
- Identify and support families experiencing homelessness in rural areas.

Final, Not Final, Thoughts

Here are final thoughts on the overall impact of homelessness on parents and children from Melissa N when asked if homelessness had a positive or negative impact on her children:

When asked if homelessness had a positive or negative impact on my children, I would love to say that it eventually transformed into a completely positive experience. The truth is... it did not. It did, however, teach some very hard lessons about loyalty, trust, and the painfully disappointing reality of manipulation, bias, and judgment from family members, and, yes, even some service providers. This has had long-lasting traumatic effects and created a place where deep-seated resentment and anger not only festered but became a trauma response affecting so many parts of my children's lives. We all have to come to terms with this in our own way and time.

This is why I say it's not so much about forgiving other people for being who they are and doing what they believe based on their experiences and the political agendas branded into their psyches, it's about learning to forgive ourselves and doing the work to rebuild the things we can so that maybe we can be a catalyst of wisdom and change for our children, their children, and those who are struggling to survive in a system that is more broken and biased than ever. My children were three years apart and have very different attitudes and outlooks on our experiences while we were homeless. Coping mechanisms, true support, education, drive, and access to resources were critical, as well as how they choose to heal and handle that part of their lives. All of these make a monumental difference in how they perceive and interact with others, our system, their family members, relationships, and life in general.

In short, I don't believe I can say the impact on my kids was positive or negative. I believe it is a combination of both. How they pull those complex experiences together and express and utilize them depends on the child as well as the extent of what and who they remember and what role these experiences played in their lives.

Our children encounter all the stress, emotions, and struggles that we do. Sometimes they either can't or don't choose to verbalize it. Trust me on this: I missed so many cues my children were trying to give me because I was living and functioning in survival mode — fight or flight — and pushing down my own PTSD because my commitment to being the best mother with no one to truly seek advice or wisdom from did NOT make it easy on any of us.

I have been my own worst enemy and beat myself up more than ANYONE else ever could. That, to this day, is something I battle with. However, I'm learning to use it as a source of empowerment to do things differently for my son while embracing every opportunity to share my nightmare of a past.

Even if one person in the position to create positive change does so, then I can find solace in knowing it wasn't all for nothing.

I learned to forgive myself. None of us asked for this. We did the best we could with the support system we had. We paid the price and our children did as well. You must forgive yourself. Take everything that happened and use it in a positive way to make change.

* Melissa N's son is a special needs child who still lives at home.

Closing Thoughts from Diane and Diana

It's sad this book needed to be written.

It's sadder still that families are experiencing homelessness at an unprecedented rate as we enter the second quarter of the 21st century. It's saddest that family homelessness seems unimportant and invisible for many policymakers and too many of us in the public.

As authors of this unique guide, we deeply appreciate the Melissas' willingness to contribute their unfettered wisdom to this project. Hopefully, as the book gets circulated to our nation's families living in similar homeless situations, the practical advice from The Three Melissas will not only provide support and encouragement but will reduce anxiety and ease tensions for families and for those trying to help them. We also hope that professionals and policymakers will gain insights about everyday logistical challenges families experiencing homelessness encounter and turn those insights into actions that lessen family homelessness.

Those of us with a place to live and the resources necessary to acquire our daily needs (and more) have a moral obligation to do what we can to ease the immediate and long-term suffering of those around us — especially those without a place to call home. In some cases, you may extend kindness and understanding. We hope that, at the very least, you'll refrain from judgment and harsh words. Perhaps you'll find a way to lend a hand, bringing comfort where none existed. For those of you who are policymakers, or those with connections to these decision-makers, you might use your position to reduce hardship and increase assistance.

Housing is a human right. Adhering to that concept would vastly improve life for those without housing, including millions of babies, toddlers, children, youth, and parents. We will collectively do better when our sisters and brothers have their basic needs met.

Family well-being requires the mutual focus and unwavering effort of a nation that values human life and believes in the potential of each person. The unconditional love of a mother toward her children is a perfect model. The Three Melissas have done their part. Now it's up to us.

The Three Melissas

Extras The Make This Handbook Even More Worthwhile

Tip Sheet for Hosts
Sharing Housing with a Family Experiencing Homelessness

You are a kind and compassionate person who wants to help a family member or a friend and their kids who have lost their housing. You have invited them to move in with you temporarily. Oftentimes, these arrangements are made quickly, before either you or your family member or friend has thought about what this means. Living together is not easy, especially if it's a situation that was not planned for.

This tip sheet will help you understand what both families will be facing and help you manage expectations to make the best of the situation.

"We have nowhere else to go…"

When a family becomes homeless, they lose more than a roof over their heads. Their world turns into chaos as they lose track of their belongings, suffer financial ruin, experience hunger and deprivation, and feel embarrassment and shame. Their trauma can result in depression and confusion, especially as parents try to protect and provide for their children. They need help with housing and basic needs, but they also need compassion and support. As a host sharing your home, you can be that safe port in the storm as the family works to regain stability.

Tips for sharing your home:

- Avoid judgment. Homelessness results from a myriad of causes, some which people can control and some which they cannot. This is not the time to question the circumstances of the family you want to help. They need housing and your compassion.
- Treat your guest family with respect. You are helping them out, but you should not talk to them in a way that makes them feel demeaned or unwelcome.
- Expect the family to treat you, your family, and your home with respect.
- Ensure that the space the family will be using is adequate for the number of people staying there and is safe and comfortable.
- Sit down with the parent/s and older children to discuss expectations. Here are some issues to cover:
  - » Where will the family be staying? Will they have their own space? Will they have access to the whole house, the living room, the kitchen, and the bathroom? Can they watch TV? Use the internet?

- Are there times when they cannot use specific areas, such as the kitchen, living room, or bathroom?
- Can they do their laundry at your house?
- Is there space for them to store their belongings beyond what they need on a day-to-day basis?
- Will the family need a locked space for valuables?
- Will they eat separately from your family?
- Will they be expected to share the cost for food? Or keep their food separate? Where can they store their food?
- Will they be expected to share the cost of household bills?
- Is smoking allowed? Use of alcohol, marijuana, or other drugs?
- Can they have guests?
- What do you expect in terms of keeping the house clean and neat?
- In what other ways can the family be helpful?
- Must their children be supervised at all times? When must the children be quiet or out of the way?
- Will you or your family members be

allowed to speak to the guest's children if they are doing something wrong? Will the guest be allowed to speak to your children if they are doing something wrong?

» Are the family's pets allowed?
» Are there particular needs or concerns that the family would like to discuss at this time? Is there a reasonable way to address these needs or concerns? (If not, this may be the time to determine whether or not this shared housing arrangement is the best option for the host family or the guest family.)

You should take notes on this discussion, keep a copy for yourself and provide a copy for your guest. This document will be a good reminder of what you discussed and will make sure that everyone is on the same page.

- Have follow-up sessions to "clear the air" as needed. It's not a bad idea to have a formal "check-in" on a weekly basis. Keeping the lines of communication open is essential to prevent annoyances from becoming conflicts.
- Discuss how long you will allow the family to stay with you. Help them plan for what comes after this time.

Tip Sheet for Parents

Staying in Someone's Home When You Have Lost Your Housing

You have lost your housing, and you are desperate to find a place where you and your children can stay temporarily. A friend, family member, or even someone you don't know has offered you a place to stay in their house for a while. Is this a good idea? Will you wear out your welcome?

Living with another person or family is not easy, especially if it's a situation that is not planned for. This tip sheet will help you be a good guest, advocate for your needs, and clarify expectations for both you and your host.

Questions for determining if a temporary doubled-up living situation is right for you and your family:

- How well to you know your host? Is this someone you trust? Is this someone you trust around your children? Is this someone you believe will not force you to do unwanted, illegal, or unsafe things as a condition for staying there (like having sex with them or trafficking drugs)?
- How well do your children know the host or host family? Are they comfortable with them?
- Is the space your host is offering to

you adequate for your family — not overcrowded, comfortably furnished with the basics, with appropriate heating and cooling, and with access to a bathroom and kitchen?
- Will you be able to organize and store your belongings? Can you lock up valuable things?
- Will your children have space to play and do their schoolwork?
- Is the home near transportation, or do you have a car to enable you to get to work and run errands?
- What can you contribute to the household while you are staying there?
- How long do you think you'll need to stay there? Do you have a plan for getting permanent housing?
- What is your plan if things don't work out and you have to move out quickly?

Tips for being a good guest:

- Be agreeable and respectful, but expect to be treated with respect in return.
- Keep the lines of communication open; when you feel like your host is crossing the line or when you feel like your host is

unhappy with you and your family being there, speak up.
- Be organized and clean up after yourself and your family — and others in the household.
- Offer to help with household chores and expenses.
- Minimize the disruption in your host's home; make sure your kids behave. Find activities to do outside of the home as much as possible.

Tips for keeping the lines of communication open:

- Before you move in, sit down with your host to discuss expectations. Here are some issues to cover:

  » Where will you be staying? Will you and your kids have your own space? Will you have access to the whole house, the living room, the kitchen, and the bathroom? Can you watch TV? Use the internet?

  » Are there times when you and your kids cannot use specific areas, such as the kitchen, living room, or bathroom?

- » Can you do laundry at your host's house?
- » Is there space for you to store your belongings?
- » Will you be able to lock up any valuables?
- » Will you and your kids eat separately from the host's family?
- » Will you be expected to share the cost for food? Or keep your food separate? Where can you store your food?
- » Will you be expected to share the cost of household bills?
- » Is smoking allowed? Use of alcohol, marijuana, or other drugs?
- » Can you or your kids have guests?
- » What does your host expect in terms of keeping the house clean and neat?
- » In what other ways can you and your kids be helpful?
- » Must you supervise your children at all times?
- » When must your children be quiet or out of the way?
- » Will you allow your host to speak to your children if they are doing

something wrong? Will you be allowed to speak to your host's children if they are doing something wrong?

- » Will your family's pets be allowed?
- » Are there particular needs or concerns that you or your host would like to discuss at this time? Is there a reasonable way to address these needs or concerns? (If not, this may be the time to determine that this shared housing arrangement is not the best option for your family or your host.)

- Take notes on this discussion, keep a copy for yourself and provide a copy for your host. This document will be a good reminder of what you discussed and will make sure that everyone is on the same page.
- Have follow-up conversations to "clear the air" as needed. Listen carefully, and ask for specific things you and your kids can do to make the living situation better.
- Have a formal "check-in" on a weekly basis. Keeping the lines of communication open is essential to prevent annoyances from becoming conflicts.

- Discuss how long your host will allow you to stay. Explain your plan for making this situation as temporary as possible.
- Show your gratitude. Opening up your home to another family is a big deal — acknowledge this.

Resources for Parents

When looking for information and resources, your best bet is to see what is available locally. Contacts at schools (school social workers and homeless liaisons), housing and social service agencies, non-profits, and churches can direct you to resources in your area. If you can't find the help you need locally, the following list of national contacts will help you or help you find other resources in your area.

Educational Services for Children and Youth Experiencing Homelessness

National Center for Homeless Education:

>nche.ed.gov
>toll-free Helpline: 800-308-2145
>homeless@serve.org

The National Center for Homeless Education (NCHE) is the U.S. Department of Education's technical assistance center to help schools and families get services and support for children experiencing homelessness. The website has information on rights and services for children and youth under the McKinney-Vento Act. If you contact NCHE on the helpline or by email, staff will help address challenges you may be facing enrolling your kids and getting educational services for your for them.

Schoolhouse Connection

schoolhouseconnection.org

SchoolHouse Connection (SHC) is a national non-profit organization that focuses on the educational needs of children and youth experiencing homelessness. Their work includes advocacy and practical assistance to early childhood programs, schools, colleges and universities, service providers, families, and youth. SHC offers many briefs and reports on various aspects of child and youth homelessness and ways that schools and communities can support the needs of children and youth who are homeless.

Educational Services for Children with Special Needs

Center for Parent Information Resource Centers

www.parentcenterhub.org

The Center for Parent Information and Resources (CPIR) is a central resource for Parent Training and Information Centers and Community Parent Resource Centers. It offers information to assist families of children with disabilities from birth to age 26 and with all types of disabilities. You can also find the Community Parent Resource Center in your area: www.parentcenterhub.org/find-your-center/

Community Parent Resource Centers are operated by local parent organizations and will help you get the training and information you need to help your children.

Childhood Trauma

National Child Traumatic Stress Network:

> www.nctsn.org

The National Child Traumatic Stress Network provides information and training materials to help people better understand the impacts of trauma and stress on children. Materials include those that can help you understand your child's reaction to traumatic events and help them recover from traumatic events.

Domestic Violence Support

National Domestic Violence Helpline:

> www.thehotline.org

The National Domestic Violence Helpline is available by calling 1-800-799-SAFE (7233), online chat, or texts for free, confidential advice related to your situation.

Mental Health Support

SAMHSA Mental Health Helpline

www.samhsa.gov/find-help/national-helpline
call 1-800-662-HELP (4357)

SAMHSA's National Helpline is a free, confidential, 24/7, 365-day-a-year treatment referral and information service (in English and Spanish) for individuals and families facing mental and/or substance use disorders. You can get a referral to local treatment facilities, support groups, and community-based organizations.

Suicide and Crisis Lifeline

Call or text 988

The Suicide and Crisis Lifeline offers free, 24/7 confidential support to anyone in suicidal or emotional distress. You will be connected to a trained crisis counselor to talk about your problems.

Legal Problems
No Easy Answers

Poverty and Legal Issues

Besides the obvious and sadly typical problems that accompany poverty and homelessness, legal dilemmas push things over the edge. If you need an example, just check out the following link with real-life scenarios that illustrate how one small incident can escalate to an insurmountable challenge. Poor, Not Guilty (poornotguilty.org/challenges.html) is an interactive website that conveys how a simple infraction can change your life for the worst.

Especially for people mired in poverty and homelessness, resources don't come close to meeting the need when it comes to basic human necessities. Picture someone who fell into a 20-foot hole being offered a broken-down 10-foot ladder—if they're lucky. Being without resources makes you extremely vulnerable when it comes to legal entanglements.

While the information in this section is not legal advice, we hope that the suggestions are useful, and the links will point you toward local resources that can help in your particular situation.

Criminalization of Homelessness

When you and your family have nowhere to sleep, much less live, you are at great risk of being charged with criminal offenses. As of the writing of this book (2024), many states and communities have laws that criminalize homelessness, which penalize you for doing things that you have few or no other options to avoid. Being unfamiliar with local laws and policies can result in fines, charges, court appearances (and fees), and other untold hardships that often lead you deeper into the criminal justice system, making it even harder to escape homelessness.

When you tumble into homelessness, the last thing on your mind is researching to find out what things are legal or not. Nevertheless, you may need to know what the laws are related to loitering, camping, sleeping in public places, or parking your car overnight, for example. Getting legal help once you need it is almost impossible. Our best advice is try to avoid any legal problems.

Here are some ways you can find the information you need:

- Research municipal ordinances on the city's or town's public website related to specific topics, such as camping or loitering.
- Search online for recent news stories about people experiencing homelessness

in your area being arrested.
- Contact someone with the homeless or housing coalition in your state or city.
- Contact a legal aid organization in your area.
- Contact the homeless liaison at your child's school who may be able to direct you to other informational resources.

Even with information, you may not be completely protected. Sometimes localities will "crack down" on homelessness on a whim, or a particular law enforcement person may be having a bad day. You just never know.

The following website offers a list of organizations for each state that may help with homelessness, legal assistance, and eviction support:
- Just Shelter
  justshelter.org/community-resources/

Other Risky Situations

Camping

We know it's not really camping. It's putting up a tent or other form of inadequate, temporary shelter for you and your family to sleep in places where it may or may not be legal for you to stay because you don't have a place to live.

Be warned! More and more states are making it illegal to "camp" on public property. In many cases, it's illegal to camp on private property. We can't give you specific details because the laws are different everywhere.

Find out as much information as you can beforehand. Even then, you should keep your valuables (IDs, important papers, anything that's not replaceable) with you. Be prepared to move out at a moment's notice.

Loitering

One of the biggest challenges for parents who are homeless, particularly those with young children, is finding a place to go when you must leave the shelter during the day. Loitering is unlawful in many communities. Even more challenging, definitions of what is considered loitering vary from community to community. Loitering can cover activities such as sleeping on a park bench or staying a long time in a store or restaurant. Some parents take their children to public libraries, which, in many communities, are lenient toward people who are homeless.

Your best bet is when you are staying for a longer-than-normal a period of time in a public place, store, or restaurant with your child, stay under the radar. Do not draw attention to yourself. And, if you are asked to leave, do so without argument. You may be within your rights, but it's not worth getting involved with law enforcement.

Eviction

Evictions often lead to homelessness, if not immediately, eventually. Unfortunately, the resources to help people facing eviction don't come close to meeting the desperate needs of households being evicted, legally or not.

Each state and municipality will have different laws, so information on how to fight evictions or determine if eviction laws in your community are being followed depends on your location. It will take research and persistence.

Your community's housing or homeless coalition or legal aid organization, if they exist, may be a good place to start. The following resource answers more general questions about eviction:

- Eviction Lab: Questions
  evictionlab.org/questions/

Order of Protection (Restraining Order)

Domestic violence is a major cause of family homelessness. Many people seek a protective order or restraining order, which is a legal document to prohibit your abuser from coming near you or harassing you or your children. You can seek a protective order at a courthouse. Keep in mind, however, that a protective order is only as effective as your abuser's willingness to follow the order or law enforcement's willingness to enforce the order. It is NOT a safety plan. You need a safety plan.

The following link is for the National Domestic Violence Hotline's for information on protective orders and safety plans: https://www.thehotline.org. You may also call: 800-799-SAFE (7233).

Child Welfare Involvement

The most common fear of parents when their families become homeless is child welfare authorities swooping in and taking custody of their children. Plenty of confusion exists about whether or not homelessness is a reason to remove children from parents. It does happen. And while sometimes it may be for the best, most often other solutions would be better for all involved.

In a perfect world, welfare agencies would

be able to support a family when they are at risk of homelessness. This can and does happen in places, but it's not a common reality. Some communities have strong protections for family stability, with welfare workers dedicated to helping families get through tough times. Don't count on that.

The most you can do is to try to avoid involvement with child welfare agencies. Do your best to take care of your children in these hard times. Always make sure your children are fed, clean, dressed appropriately for the weather, and never left alone if they are too young. Know that your best efforts might not be seen as enough.

Try to locate an agency or a knowledgeable advocate to guide you, especially if you've been contacted by child welfare authorities. The homeless liaison at your children's school may be helpful. Do your best not to panic and make decisions that might cause more problems.

Falling for Scams

Now more than ever, "deals" and offers to "help" abound, online and in-person. While some are legit, too many are scams. The last thing you need is to be scammed, which can deplete your meager resources and make you even more vulnerable to legal problems.

As with our advice above, we cannot possibly cover the many ways to avoid problems that will come at you looking like good things. It's extremely hard to be vigilant every moment while you're trying to care for your kids and get yourselves out of this bad situation.

Scammers count on you not being willing to go to the police to report someone ripping you off—the "landlord" who really doesn't own the apartment you just rented, the seller of the bogus goods you just bought, the "business owner" who refuses to pay you for the work you did, etc.

Keep in mind, if something sounds too good to be true, it probably is. If unbelievable help comes your way, be wary. Scammers prey upon desperation. Remember that you are stressed and exhausted, and you may not be thinking clearly. And, above all, don't make any snap decisions! Discuss any unexpected "opportunity" with someone you trust whose judgment is fairly sound, and see what they think. Another person's perspective is critical.

The Three Melissas

The Big Picture
by Diana and Diane

Have the Melissas in this book overcome immense obstacles to raise their children during their times of homelessness? Yes, they have.

Are the Melissas' situations unique? No, they are not.

Here is an overview of family homelessness in America, particularly homelessness among single mothers with children. We will describe the scope of the problem and the pervasive challenges that make it difficult for families experiencing homelessness to get back on their feet.

These challenges must be addressed by policy changes. Schools, service organizations, communities, and the government must implement changes to improve the lives of people in poverty in the U.S. to prevent them from becoming homeless or enable them to quickly regain financial and housing stability so that they might avoid the continuing poverty, struggle, and trauma that can impact adults and children for the rest of their lives.

Rising Numbers of Families and Children Experiencing Homelessness

Perhaps at no time in modern American history has family homelessness reached such a defining moment. Factors that contribute to homelessness—soaring rents, unprecedented evictions, record job losses, inadequate health care, for-profit housing market shifts, cost-of-living increases, etc., —have exceeded crisis levels.

Statistically, families experiencing homelessness are the fastest-growing unhoused population in the U.S. In the 2020-2021 school year, public schools identified 1,099,221 students experiencing homelessness. According to the National Center for Homeless Education, this represents 2.2% of all students enrolled in public schools, and this number has risen steadily for over 20 years.

Still, this percentage may be only a fraction of students defined as homeless. Experts have estimated that, overall, K-12 student homelessness is vastly undercounted. A 2022 Center for Public Integrity analysis of district-level federal education data suggests roughly 300,000 students experiencing homelessness have slipped through the cracks, unidentified by the school districts mandated to help them (DiPierro). Nevertheless, the staggering number of families in a variety of homeless situations reflects shamefully on our nation's family values. Making it worse is the extent of deep poverty facing tens of millions of families who teeter at the cusp of homelessness.

As significant as the above numbers are, far more young children — those under the age of six — experience homelessness. The number of preschool-aged children, infants, and toddlers experiencing homelessness in the U.S. is high. The latest data from the U.S. Department of Education (2021) shows that approximately 1.3 million children or 5% of children under the age of six experienced homelessness in the U.S. in 2018-2019. These figures represent only those experiencing homelessness who are served in school districts with McKinney-Vento subgrants. Many preschool-aged children are not. And those kids aren't on any count.

The far-reaching impacts of homelessness on all children leave lasting scars. The devastating impact of homelessness on babies and toddlers— children in their most critical period of mental and physical development— can create additional hardships for them well into adulthood. A study from Health Affairs showed that children who experienced homelessness as infants had higher incidences of respiratory infections, fever, allergies, low birthweight, injuries, and developmental disorders than other children living in poverty. The study also found that very young children who are homeless experience adverse physical consequences as well – including developmental delays. In a 2012 landmark report, the Harvard Center for the Developing Child showed that toxic stress from adverse childhood experiences, such as homelessness, can alter the structure of the brain, placing a child at risk for developing a variety of chronic, lifelong physical and mental health and learning challenges. A 2021 study showed that the experience of homelessness in childhood or youth is associated with lower odds of experiencing housing stability, suggesting the importance of intervening early in order to prevent later poor health and negative social outcomes.

Preventing babies and toddlers (and their families) from experiencing homelessness is a wise investment not just for families but for communities as well.

Parents Struggle to Get By

Recent complicating factors, such as inflation, the COVID-19 pandemic, lack of affordable housing, and other economic and societal challenges have exacerbated a rise in the number of those in poverty. Approximately one-third of Americans lived in poverty in 2021 as reported by the Poor People's Campaign on their 2023 National Fact Sheet.

In the post-pandemic era, rollbacks of safety

nets, such as SNAP and eviction protections, continue to stack the dice against low-wage workers or those unable to work. In addition, in 2022, nearly 41% of adults struggled with medical debt, with 80% of the debt belonging to households with zero or negative worth. Many parents in poverty face unimaginable challenges trying to get back on their feet while caring for their children, placing them in a vulnerable position greatly at risk of losing their housing.

Even parents with low-income jobs are unable to attain or maintain stable housing. In 2023, the National Low Income Housing Coalition reported that "In no state, metropolitan area, or county in the U.S. can a worker earning the federal or prevailing state or local minimum wage afford a modest two-bedroom rental home at fair market rent by working a standard 40-hour work week." Now, more than ever, families living in poverty, unable to save money, are often one lost paycheck, one illness, one car repair, or one family conflict away from losing their housing.

In addition, a dire shortage of affordable housing results in high rents, which impacts both middle- and low-income families. Even when housing is available, low-income parents are frequently rent-burdened, meaning that they must pay more than 30% of their income toward housing. They must juggle their income to pay bills and meet the needs of their children, often falling behind in their rent as they cascade toward eviction.

Subsidized housing continues to fall woefully short of the need. The National Low Income Housing Coalition reported that in 2021, federal housing subsidies reached an estimated 25% of those needing help to afford housing. Without government assistance, families are at the mercy of the largely unregulated private housing market. The other major homelessness factor—evictions—skyrocketed during and after the pandemic. With an eviction on your record, finding a place to rent becomes almost impossible.

Systemic racism continues to prevent people of color from accessing housing, employment, education, and adequate health care. According to the 2023 Poor People's Campaign, the disparity in the poverty rates between white people (25%), and people of color, including Black people (48%), Latino/Hispanic (52%), and people who identify as "other" (34%), is staggering. Not surprisingly, there are also higher rates of homelessness among people of color. For example, in 2022 in the U.S. people who identified as Black made up 12% of the total population but comprised 37% of all people experiencing homelessness.

Most parents of infants and toddlers struggle to find childcare or early childhood programs for their children. Preschools, such as Head Start, can be a critical buffer to the impact of homelessness on young children. They also assist educators in identifying developmental problems before the child starts school. As with other resources serving homeless and near-homeless families, many areas don't have these programs. If they do, they may have waiting lists.

A 2022 study of 20 states from SchoolHouse Connection showed that only 7% of infants and toddlers experiencing homelessness were enrolled in an early childhood program, such as *Early Head Start, Child Care*, or *Parents as Teachers Home Visiting*. Most parents who are homeless must rely on informal childcare, such as relatives, friends, or neighbors because informal childcare arrangements are less expensive and can help when parents are working odd hours or shift work. However, informal childcare arrangements are often short term and less reliable, causing parents to miss work. Additionally, young children may falter at the hands of people who, at best, are babysitting and providing only minimal oversight and stimulation.

The Typical First "Option" Doubling Up

Most communities, especially in non-urban areas, lack sufficient emergency shelters or appropriate alternative assistance when families lose housing. If a community has a shelter, other factors can create barriers that make staying there unfeasible. Two-parent families (female/male) are frequently not allowed. Same-sex couples face even more barriers. Teens, especially teenage boys, are commonly denied access with their families. Occasionally, male teens are accepted in adult male shelters. But unaccompanied teens sheltered with unsupervised adults is ill-advised for myriad reasons.

Many shelters close at daybreak, requiring everyone to leave until nightfall. Consequently, single parents without childcare options, as well as families and individuals suffering from illness, have nowhere to convalesce while they are ill. Unrealistic time limits, religious requirements, and/or curfews that conflict with work schedules make shelters less than ideal for many individuals and families.

Consequently, most parents who are homeless seek accommodations other than shelters. They will search for a relative or friend or — when truly desperate — a stranger who will allow them and their children to stay at their home for any period of time. The National Center for Homeless Education reported that in the 2019-20 school year, 77% of children identified as homeless were living doubled up due to lack of housing while only 11% stayed in homeless shelters or transitional housing.

While living doubled up means that a parent and their children who have lost their housing have a roof over their heads, living doubled up is an often unstable, traumatic, and dangerous existence. The McKinney-Vento Act includes in its definition of homeless *children living in shared housing (aka doubling up) due to the loss of their housing* because of its negative impacts on children and families.

Moreover, families experiencing homelessness who live in doubled-up situations are more hidden and harder to link to services. Commonly, they don't realize that staying with others constitutes homelessness. Some parents experience shame about their living situation or — often not the best situation — desperate adults may fear losing their children to child protective services. Most private leases do not allow for additional tenants (not on the lease) to visit for extended periods of time, putting both the hosts and guests at risk of eviction.

Federally-funded housing definitely does not allow doubling up by individuals not on the lease — and an eviction from HUD housing may result in the host being permanently banned from assisted housing.

Even when the host has no barriers to increasing the number of housing occupants, tensions may run high. Parents may be reluctant to complain about abusive situations because they don't want their host to kick them out. The "normal" stresses of too many people in too small a space creates the "walking on eggshells" syndrome that many doubled-up families describe.

Some specific challenges that doubled-up living creates are:

- Lack of sufficient space—The parents and children may have one small room or common area where they sleep, keep their belongings, and stay. They may not be welcome in other parts of the house. Children may have to stay in their sleeping space for playing, homework, AND sleeping. The parents and children often sleep in one bed or on the floor.

- Chaotic living—Along with limited living and sleeping space comes limited storage space. The parents' and children's belongings are confined to a small space or may be parceled out among other friends' and relatives' homes. Children may not have their toys or sufficient clothing available. Parents may not be able to keep track of necessary documents. They may have to store their food in the room with them.

- Unfamiliar rules and routines—Living according to unfamiliar rules and routines of the household to "keep the peace" causes innumerable problems. It interferes with parenting as other people in the household may discipline the children staying with them. Parents may fear that their crying babies or active children will aggravate their host, resulting in eviction. Not all adults or older children in the home are "safe," resulting in the guest parent's hyper-vigilance to protect their children, putting inordinate stress on both the parents and children.

- Inevitable conflicts—Conflicts often arise when communications break down between the host and parents, especially if the host feels that the family has overstayed their welcome. The guest parents must give in to what they feel are unreasonable demands, just to stay.

- Nutrition and hygiene—The parents and children staying in the home may have to defer to the host family's priority for using the kitchen or bathroom, making the provision of regular meals or toilet activities difficult.
- Transportation—Guest parents may have found an inconveniently located host home. Whether far from work or school or public transport, this can pose a hardship to schedules for everyone. If the guests don't have a car, they may become even more reliant on the host family – people who may or may not be willing to give them rides on a continual basis.
- Degrading or dangerous demands – Sadly, many women who are staying with men, either an acquaintance or sometimes a stranger, are expected to provide sex. People with no housing options may have to barter their bodies to keep a roof over their children's heads. They may also struggle to keep their children from witnessing this behavior.

Challenges for Single Mothers Experiencing Homelessness

Poverty rates for families headed by single mothers greatly exceed those of other families. The Annie E. Casey Foundation reported that, in 2021, nearly 30% of single parents lived in poverty while just 6% of married couples fit this same statistic. Single parents are also more likely to live in poverty when compared to cohabiting couples, and single mothers are much more likely to be poor compared to single fathers.

Single mothers have a higher risk of homelessness for a variety of reasons:

- Discrimination: Despite fair-housing laws, single-woman-headed households may be prohibited or discouraged from renting due to the number of children in their household, gender of their children, or pregnancy. They may be prevented from renting smaller, affordable units due to occupancy limits. They may lack adequate credit, or their credit history may be tarnished by previous experiences and/or relationships.

- Employment and childcare challenges: Many single mothers without access to childcare are unable to obtain employment. Young children may not be safe in their living situation and many moms miss work to protect their children. Additionally, illness or injury to the mother or child may result in missing work.

- Lack of education and training: Many mothers without childcare have been unable to complete or follow up on educational and training opportunities to increase their employability and income.

- Domestic violence or intimate partner abuse: Mothers often endure abusive relationships to keep a roof over their children's heads. Leaving an abuser often means leaving without housing options. Homelessness is preferable when the danger becomes too great.

- Depression or other mental health issues: Traumatic events and the many stressors on single mothers living in poverty can result in unmet mental healthcare needs, making it difficult to function and navigate complex systems or seek assistance.

- Physical health issues: Poverty, trauma, physical and mental abuse, inadequate nutrition, and a host of other issues force mothers to contend with debilitating health problems and they often lack medical care. Poor physical health may jeopardize their ability to adequately care for their family.

What This Means for Survival

All mothers, to the best of their ability, will do whatever is necessary to provide for their children. Since the beginning of time, mothers have sacrificed their health, safety, and well-being to make sure their children's needs are met. As challenges escalate, so do the mothers' efforts, often putting them at great risk mentally and physically.

While experiencing the devastating effects of homelessness, single mothers, like the Melissas, use ingenuity and fortitude to meet their children's needs. They protect their children at all costs in a society that works against them – putting barriers in their way.

It would be fair to ask policymakers why those most vulnerable families should face the greatest challenges to survival. What is gained by discarding these parents and their children? It seems we lose untapped potential and waste the resources offered to society by millions of parents and their children.

*For a more personal understanding of the challenges that parents and children experiencing homelessness face every day, visit the **HEAR US** website. (hearus.us) HEAR US is a unique, effective national nonprofit organization dedicated to giving voice and visibility to families and youth experiencing homelessness. View Diane's classic film **My Own Four Walls** to hear children tell their stories.*

References and Suggested Reading

Annie E. Casey Foundation. (June 23, 2023). Child well-being in single parent families. https://www.aecf.org/blog/child-well-being-in-single-parent-families#:~:text=In%202021%2C%20nearly%2030%25%20of,poor%20compared%20to%20single%20fathers.

Aurand, A., Emmanuel, D., Threet, D., Rafi, I., Yentel, D. (2021, March). *Gap: A shortage of affordable homes.* National Low-Income Housing Coalition. https://reports.nlihc.org/sites/default/files/gap/Gap-Report_2021.pdf

Barnes, S. G. (2022, September 22). Census data proves anti-poverty measures work. Institute for Policy Studies. https://otherwords.org/census-data-proves-anti-poverty-measures-work/

Clark, R.E., Weinreb, L., Flahive, J.M., & Seifert, R.W. (2019, May). Infants exposed to homelessness: Health, health care use, and health spending from birth to age six. *Health Affairs.* 38 (5). https://www.healthaffairs.org/doi/pdf/10.1377/hlthaff.2019.00090

Di Pierro, A., Mitchell, C. (2022, November 15). Hidden toll: Thousands of schools fail to count homeless. Center for Public Integrity. https://www.chalkbeat.org/2022/11/15/23452172/homeless-children-in-america-family-homelessness-students-mckinney-vento-act-statistics/#:~:text=And%20many%20more%20districts%20are,with%20unstable%20housing%20can%20be.

Haskett, M. E., Armstrong, J. M., & Tisdale, J. (2016). Developmental status and social-emotional functioning of young children experiencing homelessness. *Early Childhood Education Journal, 44*(2), 119–125. https://doi.org/10.1007/s10643-015-0691-8

Lopes, L., Kearney, A., Montero, A., Hamel, L., Brodie, M. (2022, June 16). *Health care debt in the U.S.: The broad consequences of medical and dental bills.* The Kaiser Foundation. https://www.kff.org/report-section/kff-health-care-debt-survey-main-findings/

National Center for Homeless Education (NCHE). (2022). *Student homelessness in America: School years 2018-19 to 2020-21.* https://nche.ed.gov/wp-content/uploads/2022/11/Student-Homelessness-in-America-2022.pdf

National Low Income Housing Coalition. (2023). *Out of reach: The high cost of housing.* https://nlihc.org/oor

Parpouchi, M., Moniruzzaman, A., & Somers, J.M. (2021, March 8). The association between experiencing homelessness in childhood or youth and adult housing stability in Housing First. *BMC Psychiatry.* 21, Article number 138. https://bmcpsychiatry.biomedcentral.com/articles/10.1186/s12888-021-03142-0

Poor People's Campaign. (2023). National Fact Sheet. https://www.poorpeoplescampaign.org/wp-content/uploads/2023/06/2023-National-Fact-Sheet-Template_6-4-8.5-×-11-in-updated.pdf

SchoolHouse Connection. (2022, November). *Infants and toddlers experiencing homelessness: Prevalence & access to early learning in twenty states.* https://schoolhouseconnection.org/wp-content/uploads/2022/11/SHC_Infant-and-Toddler-Homelessness_2022.pdf

Shonkoff, J.P. & Garner, A.S. (2012, January). The lifelong effects of early childhood adversity and toxic stress. *Pediatrics.* 129(1). 232-246. https://publications.aap.org/pediatrics/article/129/1/e232/31628/The-Lifelong-Effects-of-Early-Childhood-Adversity?autologincheck=redirected

Smith, S. K. & McCarty, C. (2011, Fall). Housing damage and population displacement during Florida's 2004 hurricane season. *Journal of Florida Studies.* 1(1). https://www.journaloffloridastudies.org/housingdamage.html

Vissing, Y. & Nilan, D. & Hudson, C. (2020). Changing the paradigm of homelessness. Routledge. https://www.routledge.com/Changing-the-Paradigm-of-Homelessness-1st-Edition/Vissing-Nilan-Hudson/p/book/9781138362987

Yamashiro, A. & McLaughlin, J. (2021). *Early childhood homelessness state profiles.* U.S. Department of Education. https://www2.ed.gov/rschstat/eval/disadv/homeless/early-childhood-homelessness-state-profiles-2021.pdf

Acknowledgements

We are so grateful for all who have helped to make our unique vision for this book a reality. The following people read an early draft and encouraged us, and they offered some great suggestions: Julia Jilek, Principal (retired), Alternative School, White Bear Lake, MN; Sue Wanzer, advisory analyst, Blowing Rock, NC; Mary Haskett, Professor Emeritus, NC State University, Raleigh, NC; and Eleanor Bader, freelance journalist, Brooklyn, NY.

We received additional positive feedback and thoughtful comments from the following reviewers who read a later draft: Deborah Gilbert White, PhD, author of Beyond Charity: A Sojourner's Reflections on Homelessness, Advocacy, Empowerment and Hope and Director of Education for the National Coalition for the Homeless, Washington, D.C.; Jennifer M. Kassebaum, owner of Flint Hills Books, Council Grove, KS; Dana Malone, MA, New Mexico State Coordinator, Education for Homeless Children and Youth Program, Santa Fe, NM; and Judd Lofchie, attorney, Lofchie & Associates, Aurora, IL.

Tremendous support came from the our publisher, the Charles Bruce Foundation, including expert editorial guidance from Pat LaMarche and Cheryl Dunn Bychek, foundation board members. Many thanks go to those who shaped our draft into an artfully designed and easy to read guidebook. The team includes Chad Bruce; Max Donnelly; and Bonnie Tweedy Shaw, Tweedy Art Unlimited.

Other behind-the-scenes supporters include our website designer Kelsey Mabry, Mabry Design, Greensboro, NC. And of course, some significant family members, including Sue and Chuck Wanzer, Diane's sister and brother-in-law, and Mike Howard, Diana's husband, who are always there whenever we need them in big and small ways.

No amount of gratitude is sufficient for the three Melissas for their wisdom and honesty in our interviews and conversations. We feel honored that they put their trust and confidence in us to share their lived experience to help other parents survive their journeys of homelessness. This book, which gives readers a window into what it's like to be homeless with young children, provides a challenge to those of us with the wherewithal to respond to both the systemic and material real needs of families and children in these devastating circumstances.